TEACHING ELECTRICITY EFFECTIVELY:
a research-based guide for primary science

Authors: Mike Summers
             Colin Kruger
             Jenny Mant

Illustrations: Colin Kruger

Published by the Association for Science Education

ISBN: 0 86357 272 3

Acknowledgements
The authors would like to thank the Institution of Electrical Engineers and
Esso UK plc for funding this work, and the primary teachers who
participated in the research.

CONTENTS

PREFACE

This book has been written for practising primary school teachers, and for anyone concerned with inservice or preservice science teacher education.

The overall purpose of the book is to identify ways in which ideas about electricity and simple circuits can be taught effectively in primary school classrooms.

The book:

- is based on in-depth case studies of the teaching of electricity by three primary school teachers in which children's understanding was investigated before and after teaching.

- describes the subject knowledge and teaching approaches which were used to develop effectively children's understanding of this topic.

- provides detailed accounts of the teaching and of the children's learning.

The research identified:

- a set of electricity concepts which can be acquired readily by primary school teachers and taught effectively to children.

- numerous ways in which teachers can develop children's ideas successfully, and some of the pitfalls to be avoided.

The authors wish to thank the teachers who took part in these case studies for granting access to their classrooms and coping with the intrusion of video and audio recording equipment and the research team.

We also wish to thank the Institution of Electrical Engineers and Esso UK plc for funding this work.

CHAPTER 1

INVESTIGATING EFFECTIVE TEACHING

WHAT IS MEANT BY EFFECTIVE TEACHING?

It is possible to conceive of several different approaches to the identification of *effective* teaching. For example:

- teachers' own perceptions about what is effective in their work.

- children's perceptions about why they learnt particular things.

- peer judgment i.e. a particular teacher is identified by colleagues as someone who is effective.

- examination or test results.

A key feature of the research described in this book is the use of pupil learning outcomes as the principal criterion for effectiveness, and in particular *the ways in which children's ideas have changed* following teaching.

Hence, at the heart of these case studies is an investigation of children's initial understanding of the ideas to be taught and the extent to which which these have become more scientific after teaching.

However, while this was the principal criterion used for effectiveness, the opportunity was also taken during interviews with children to ask them why they learnt what they learnt. Some perceptions of the children are reported in this book, but the main emphasis is on an objective appraisal of children's learning.

TWO KEY IDEAS: SUBJECT KNOWLEDGE AND TEACHING KNOWLEDGE

The concern of the research was to identify ways in which ideas about electricity and simple circuits can be taught effectively in primary school classrooms. This book analyses effective teaching principally in terms of two types of knowledge:

- *subject knowledge* i.e. teachers' personal understanding of the subject matter they are teaching (in this case, electricity and simple circuits), and

- subject specific *teaching knowledge* i.e. knowing how to help children understand the subject matter.

Having adequate subject knowledge is clearly, for a teacher, only a first step. The professional task is to help children acquire this knowledge.

In the academic literature this latter kind of knowledge - knowing how to make ideas accessible to children - is known as pedagogical content knowledge (Shulman, 1986). In this book we prefer to use the simpler term teaching knowledge (which most of the time will be subject or even topic specific).

According to Shulman, teaching knowledge for a given topic includes knowledge of:

- the conceptions and preconceptions that children of different ages and backgrounds bring with them to the learning of a topic.

- the strategies most likely to be fruitful in reorganising the understanding of learners.

- the most useful forms of representation of ideas, the most powerful analogies, illustrations, examples, explanations and demonstrations.

The goal of the research was to identify the teacher subject knowledge and teaching knowledge which can help children develop effectively their understanding of electricity and simple circuits.

Figure 1 provides an example of the distinction between subject knowledge and teaching knowledge, albeit in contexts other than that of electricity.

Note that teaching knowledge is often topic specific rather than just subject specific. So, for example, when teaching electricity it includes knowledge of children's prior ideas *about electricity and circuits*, and of appropriate analogies for the teaching *of this particular topic*.

Identification of effective teaching knowledge is, in our view, essential for the future development of science teaching in primary schools.

| **Fig 1** | **Examples of subject knowledge and teaching knowledge** |

Forces	**Sound**
Subject knowledge: the Earth attracts all objects with a force due to gravity.	*Subject knowledge:* sounds are made when objects vibrate.
Teaching knowledge: this force can be imagined as a 'gravity-spring' joining the object to the Earth's centre.	*Teaching knowledge:* the vibration of a cymbal can be shown by scattering sand-grains on it, striking it and watching the sand-grains 'dance'.

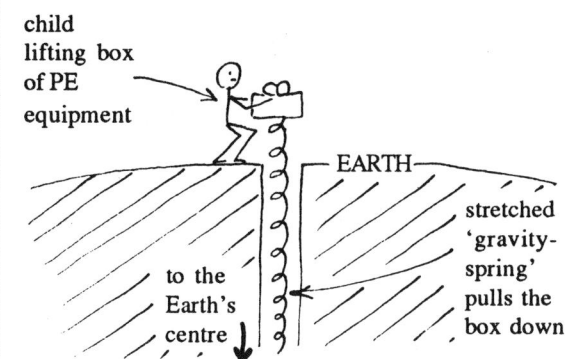

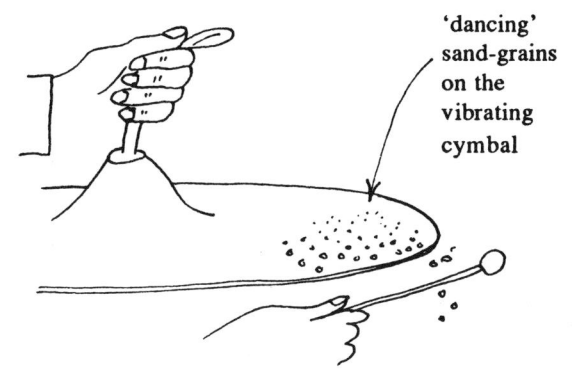

STUDYING EFFECTIVE TEACHING

The participating teachers and children

Six teachers were recruited to the project, with three of these forming the bases of the case studies. These teachers were volunteers, and only one of them had any specialist knowledge of science.

The learning of all children in the classes taught by the teachers was investigated before and after teaching using pencil and paper tests of the ideas expressed in the teachers' objectives. Since these objectives differed, the tests were tailored to cover the goals of each teacher. Some examples of the questions used are given later in this chapter.

In addition teachers were asked to select six children representing a range of abilities from each class. The learning of these children was followed in detail, using interviews based on the pencil and paper tests, pre- and post-teaching.

Stages

The research was carried out in the stages described below.

(1) A short, initial burst of inservice training was provided to help teachers develop their subject and teaching knowledge in the area of electricity and simple circuits.

This training consisted of about 16 hours of taught sessions and practical activities based on a published set of materials (Summers, Kruger and Mant, 1995), spread over three days. The teaching knowledge was not prescriptive, but rather introduced a range of perspectives on science teaching, with practical examples related to electricity, which teachers could use as a model for their own preparation and teaching. An account of the inservice training programme is given in Chapter 2.

(2) Following this INSET, teachers specified conceptual learning objectives for their pupils prior to a teaching sequence on electricity and planned how they would try to achieve these objectives. The teachers were then interviewed about their objectives and plans to ensure that these were understood clearly by the research team.

(3) Pupils' prior conceptions about the ideas to be taught were investigated systematically using pencil and paper tests with whole classes and in-depth interviews with each sub-group of six pupils.

(4) The teaching sequences were video and audio taped.

(5) Following teaching, interviews with teachers were held to gain their perspectives on whether or not their objectives were achieved and why.

(6) Finally, the ways in which children's ideas had changed following teaching were investigated by re-administering the pencil and paper tests and re-interviewing each subset of six children.

Examples of the questions used

A particular challenge for the research was the design of pencil and paper tests which could be used both *before* and after teaching. For the class of each teacher, the same test was used on both occasions, but the obvious task was to design a test which

- children could attempt *before* teaching when they might have very little knowledge about electricity and simple circuits, and

- which they would find attractive, interesting and motivating, so they would want to respond to the questions.

Because of the first of these points, the questions had to avoid or use very carefully any scientific terms which might subsequently be taught and which would discourage children from responding before teaching.

Two examples of questions used are given in Figs. 2 and 3. Further examples appear in later chapters, and a complete test used with the children of one teacher is given in Appendix 1.

Figure 2 is an example of a question which did use a scientific term (electric current) but in such a way that children felt they could (and in fact did) respond. An example of responses before and after teaching is given.

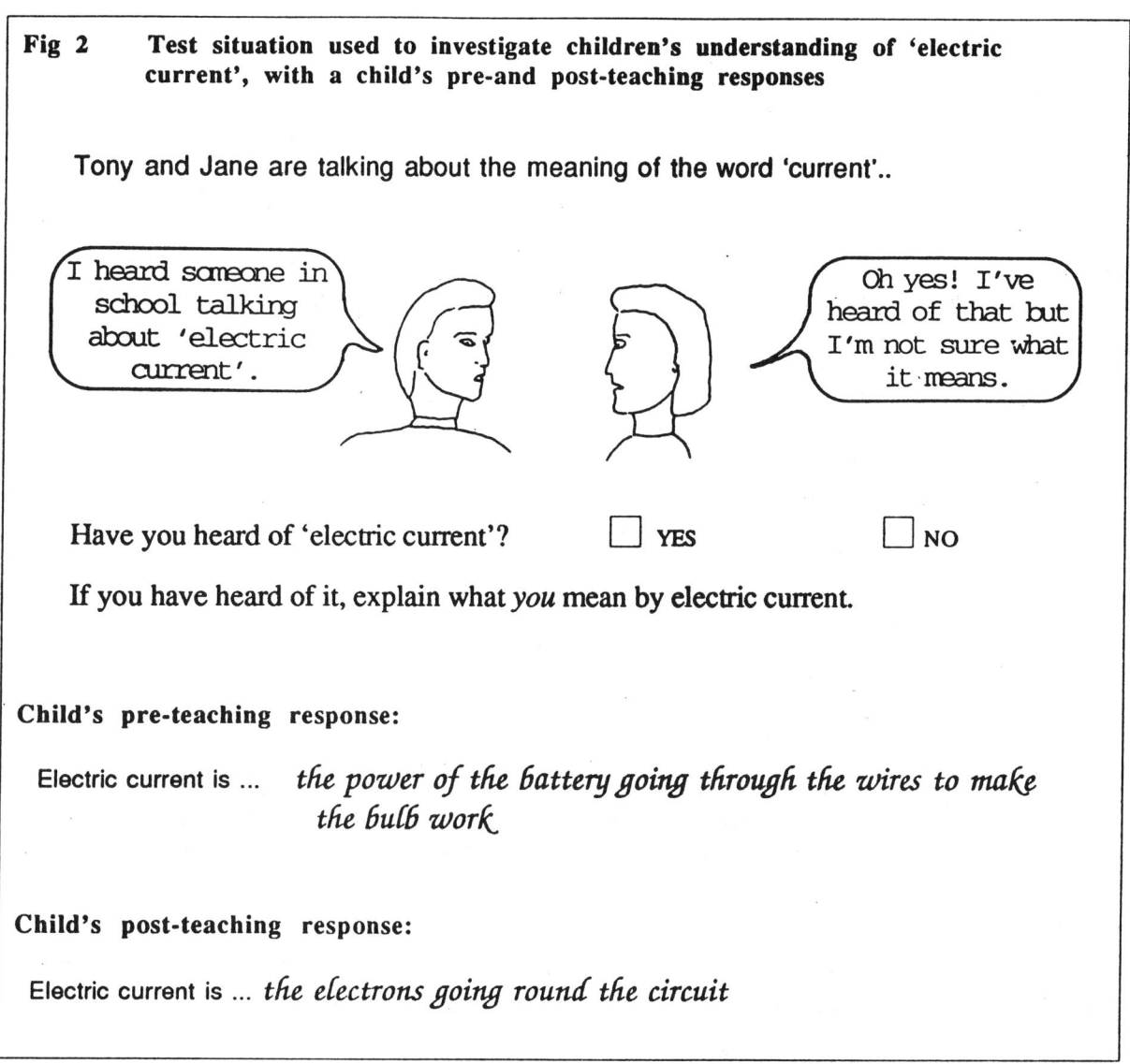

Fig 2   **Test situation used to investigate children's understanding of 'electric current', with a child's pre-and post-teaching responses**

Tony and Jane are talking about the meaning of the word 'current'..

I heard someone in school talking about 'electric current'.

Oh yes! I've heard of that but I'm not sure what it means.

Have you heard of 'electric current'?   ☐ YES   ☐ NO

If you have heard of it, explain what *you* mean by electric current.

Child's pre-teaching response:

Electric current is ... *the power of the battery going through the wires to make the bulb work*

Child's post-teaching response:

Electric current is ... *the electrons going round the circuit*

Figure 3 also includes an example of the responses from one child both before and after teaching. The kind of open-ended question seen in Fig 3 is of course more difficult to score than a closed item, and the research team had to devise carefully agreed criteria for assessing the responses (see later).

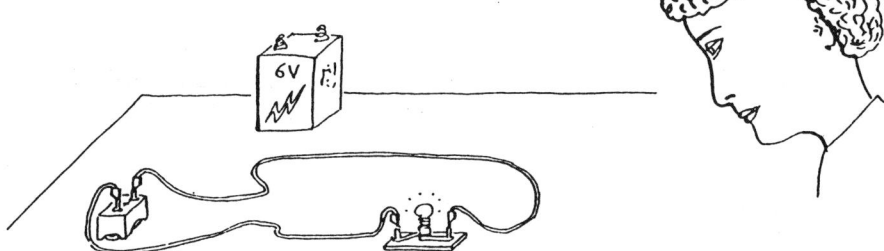

Fig 3   Test situation used to investigate children's understanding of voltage and the battery's role, with a child's pre- and post-teaching responses

The teacher has given Debbie 2 batteries to use. Debbie has connected up her circuit using this 1.5 V battery and the bulb is glowing.

When she swaps batteries and uses the 6 V battery, the bulb shines much more brightly.

Write down any ideas you have about '1.5 V' and '6 V' to explain why this happens.

Child's pre-teaching response:

6 V contains more electricity and is more powerful

Child's post-teaching response:

The 6 V has more push to move the electrons

(*Note:* 'more push' refers to an idea taught in the INSET and by the teacher to this child, namely, that an electric current consists of electrons in the wire being pushed by the battery. The battery does *not* produce these electrons - they are *already present* all round the circuit. This idea is dealt with in more detail in later chapters.)

Scoring the tests

The response to each question in a pencil and paper test was scored according to judgments made of the knowledge and understanding displayed, using the following scheme:

Score 0   little or no understanding
Score 1   partial understanding
Score 2   good understanding

Details of the scoring procedure and of the criteria used for allocating scores are given in Appendix II.

The pupil interviews

As mentioned above, six children from each class, representing a range of abilities (as judged by their teacher), were interviewed individually and in depth about the ideas expressed in their teacher's objectives. The questions and tasks used in the paper and pencil tests (which, of course, covered these objectives) were used as the focus for the interview.

So, for example, in the case of Fig. 3 the interviewer started the conversation by asking the child to explain what 'V' in the example stands for. A request was also made to explain more fully what had been written as an answer. Follow-up questions might be of the type:

- why do you think the bulb becomes brighter with the 6 V battery?

- can you tell me how you think the battery does this?

In the post-teaching interview, additional questions were asked such as:

- so what do you think you have you learned? How did you learn that?

- is there anything you think the teacher did to help you learn that?

- anything about that which you think you are still stuck on or unsure of?

Children were shown their post-teaching responses and asked to compare them with those made before teaching. Further questions were posed:

- before the lessons you thought this - now you think this - why is that?

- why (*if applicable*) do you think you have changed your idea?

The interviews, described in some detail in Chapter 6, provided far richer insights into the learning achieved than the pencil and paper tests. The in-depth nature of these interviews also meant that the understanding of the six children could be gauged with more certainty than that of children who only did the written tests.

Assessing children's understanding

All the children interviewed were allocated a score of 0, 1 or 2 from their interview responses using the same criteria as for scoring written responses in the pencil and paper tests. The in-depth nature of each interview means that considerable confidence can be placed in scores allocated from interviews. The procedures used for analysing these interviews are described in Chapter 6 and examples are shown in Appendix III.

By allocating a score from an interview and cross-checking this with the score of the same pupil on the written test, the validity of the written test as an indicator of understanding could be assessed.

An illustrative set of results showing the comparison for one group of six children (taught by Sarah: see Chapter 5) is shown in Table 1. Given that greater confidence can be placed in the interview scores, this table suggests that, on the whole, the pencil and paper tests tended to underestimate the knowledge and understanding of these children. The equivalent tables for the other two case study teachers (see Appendix IV) also show this trend. Very occasionally, however, the reverse is true i.e. the tests overestimate the interview scores. Table 1 shows that this occurs for one of Sarah's 14 objectives pre-teaching and for two objectives post-teaching. In the case of the other two teachers (see Appendix IV again), the tests overestimate the interview scores for only four of 15 objectives, and even then to only a small degree.

Table 1   **Comparison between interview and pencil and paper test scores for each objective (Teacher Sarah: mean scores of six children)**

Teacher's objectives (see Chapter 5 for details)	Pre-teaching		Post-teaching	
	Test	Interview	Test	Interview
1.	1.17	2	1.5	2
2.	0.5	1.33	1.5	2
3.	0	0	0.67	1.5
4.	0	0	1	2
5.	0	0	1.33	2
6.	0	0	1.33	1.33
7.	0	0	0.33	0
8.	0.5	0	1.17	0.67
9.	0	0	1.3	1.5
10.	1	1.17	1.17	2
11.	0.83	2	1.83	2
12.	0	0	0.5	1
13.	0	0	0.5	0.5
14.	2	2	2	2

Generally, the agreement between test and interview scores is quite striking for these two teachers (more so than for Sarah).

In the case studies of teaching presented in this book, judgments about the extent to which teaching was effective *are based on the mean paper and pencil test scores for the whole class* for each objective. The evidence presented above suggests that, on the whole, these scores are likely to have underestimated the knowledge and understanding of the children.

It should be noted that the interview data, despite its greater dependability, cannot be taken as an indicator of the learning of the whole class. Although each teacher was asked to select six children representing a range of abilities for the interviews, the research team had no control over this selection and the representative nature of these subgroups is very uncertain. Hence the interview data was used only as an indicator of the validity of the pencil and paper tests (as described above), and for the in-depth descriptions of children's learning given in Chapter 6.

Analysing the teaching

Primary classrooms are complex places - perhaps dauntingly so if the goal is to try and analyse all of this complexity. This was *not* the intention of the present research. The approach taken was to score the pupil pencil and paper tests for a given class to find out which objectives had been achieved successfully. The teaching which achieved these objectives was deemed to have been effective, in accord with the criterion for 'effective' adopted at the start of the research. The particular teaching sequences which targeted these successfully achieved objectives were then selected from the video recordings and, together with audio tapes, used as the focus for analysis.

The purpose of the analysis was to identify the subject knowledge and subject specific teaching knowledge used in these sequences, and to identify other characteristics of the teaching together with possible pitfalls and ways in which the teaching might have been further developed.

The teacher interviews

Towards the end of the inservice training sessions, the teachers had been introduced to the idea of specifying conceptual objectives for children's learning i.e. objectives expressing the concepts which children were intended to acquire as a result of teaching.

On completion of the INSET, the teachers were asked to set out in writing, in their own time, conceptual objectives for the teaching of electricity and circuits which they had agreed to undertake with their children as part of the research. They were also asked to plan in writing how they hoped to achieve these objectives.

These objectives and plans were sent to the research team, following which each teacher was interviewed to:

- clarify, if necessary, the objectives and teaching plan, and

- ensure that both teacher and the research team shared a common understanding of the objectives and teaching plan.

In addition, this pre-teaching interview provided an opportunity to probe teacher's views about:

- their confidence in teaching electricity, and reasons for this.

- the thinking which contributed to their overall planning strategy.

- how their approach to this work on electricity differed from that taken with other work.

- any particular difficulties they may have experienced in their planning.

As soon after the teaching as possible, and before the post-teaching pencil and paper tests and interviews with children, the teacher was interviewed a second time. One purpose of this interview was to obtain the teacher's own perceptions of the effectiveness of the teaching (i.e. whether their objectives were met). In addition, teachers were asked to reflect openly on their teaching and:

- explain what they thought went well.

- describe any difficulties they experienced during the teaching.

- comment on the correspondence between the cognitive level of their objectives and the age/ability of the children.

- describe the role children's misconceptions played in their teaching.

- develop any other points that arose from the lessons observed.

When the entire research procedure was completed, teachers were shown the test responses of the six children they had chosen for in-depth investigation, so that they could see for themselves the difference in these children's performance resulting from their teaching.

SUMMARY

In this chapter effective teaching has been defined in terms of pupil learning outcomes, and in particular the ways in which children's ideas have become more scientific following teaching. Two types of knowledge used by teachers were introduced, namely subject knowledge and teaching knowledge. Subject knowledge was defined as a teacher's personal understanding of the subject matter to be taught. Teaching knowledge was defined as knowing how to help children understand this subject matter. A description was given of the methods used in the research programme to identify the subject and teaching knowledge which can be used to help children develop effectively their understanding of electricity and simple circuits.

CHAPTER 2

THE INSERVICE TRAINING

INTRODUCTION

The initial phase of the research project, after the participating teachers had been recruited, was the inservice training course. This chapter is concerned with that inservice training phase. Firstly, the need for training and the training goals are considered. Then an account of the training course itself is given. The structure and content are described together with the approaches used throughout the course. Aspects of the course which led to significant learning are identified as well as those where difficulties were encountered. The chapter concludes by recounting how the teachers felt about teaching electricity after the course.

The teachers commented on their learning both informally and as part of structured exercises. They also completed an evaluation questionnaire at the end. Quotes from the teachers are used extensively throughout the chapter.

The goal is to portray a picture of the training as a whole and how the teachers reacted to it.

WHY INSET?

As described in Chapter 1, the focus of the research project was an investigation of effective teaching of electricity. Effective teaching was deemed to have taken place if the children had an improved understanding of electricity after teaching compared to their understanding before teaching. We were particularly interested in children's understanding of concepts in this area of the science curriculum and the subject knowledge and teaching knowledge which can be used to develop that understanding. Therefore the teachers needed access to, and understanding of, relevant subject knowledge and teaching knowledge in electricity before attempting to develop children's understanding.

The goals of the training related to both the teachers' learning and to the smooth operation of the research project. They were as follows:

- to develop the teachers' own understanding of the concepts and ideas in the area of electricity and simple circuits. In other words, to develop their subject knowledge.

- to introduce to the teachers a range of perspectives on science teaching, with practical examples related to electricity, which they could use as a model for their own preparation and teaching. In other words, to develop their teaching knowledge.

12

- to develop teachers' thinking about conceptual objectives i.e. objectives expressing the scientific ideas that children were to understand as a result of the teaching.

- to help the teachers gain confidence in their ability to teach electricity.

- to familiarise the teachers with the research team and build a cooperative rapport. A particular goal here was that the teachers would feel comfortable when a researcher visited their classrooms.

- to start to plan and prepare the next stage of the research project.

THE TEACHERS BEFORE TRAINING

The teachers were typical of many, probably most, primary school teachers, apart from one who had a science degree. The others were not science specialists and had little, or no, science in their background (see the case studies, chapters 3 to 5, for individual details). *All* six teachers lacked confidence in their ability to teach electricity. When asked to rate their pre-training confidence on a scale of 1 (little confidence) to 5 (very confident) three of the teachers scored 1 and three scored 2.

In discussion one teacher said she always avoided electricity herself and made sure someone else taught it. Other teachers expressed their lack of confidence and knowledge as follows:

> (I did) loads of 'Blue Peter' teaching (*see Fig 4*) last term with no reference to concepts.

> My basic understanding of most scientific concepts is very poor.

> (I have) a lack of knowledge beyond getting a bulb to light in a simple circuit.

Fig 4   'Blue Peter' teaching and teaching concepts

In 'Blue Peter' teaching, an experience is given to children just for its own sake without any attempt to influence their thinking.

> Here's a nice thing to do. With two bulbs together they are dimmer.

In teaching concepts, an experience is used to stimulate children to consider their own and others' ideas about what is happening and think of ways of investigating them.

> What do you think is happening in the wires to make the bulb dimmer?

In spite of this lack of confidence all of the teachers had volunteered to be part of the research project. They were prepared to put themselves in the situation of having a researcher in their classrooms observing them teach in an area of knowledge which was new to them. They approached the training with both enthusiasm and trepidation. Enthusiasm, because they wanted to know more about electricity and how to teach it. Trepidation, because they were worried in case they found it too difficult.

THE STRUCTURE AND CONTENT OF THE INSET

The training consisted of three full days of taught sessions. These took place on one day a week for three consecutive weeks. Between sessions there were reading and self assessment activities to do at home. The whole training course was based on a published set of materials written for primary teacher education as part of an earlier research project (Summers, Kruger and Mant 1995).

The course was in three parts. One of the training days was devoted to each of these parts. Part 1 covered electricity and simple circuits; Part 2 introduced and used some additional components; and Part 3 was about the teaching of electricity.

Part 1 introduced the ideas and concepts involved in the scientific view of electricity and simple circuits, and focused on developing the teachers' understanding of these. It started with a familiar activity in which the teachers had to make a bare bulb light using just a battery and lengths of wire (the 'scissors and sellotape approach') . Battery and bulb holders with plug-in leads were then introduced and used. Although it was important for the teachers to gain experience in building simple circuits, the main emphasis of this part of the course was on the scientific explanations for what constitutes electricity and for what is happening in an electric circuit. The concepts of electricity as electrons, electron flow as electric current, voltage as a measure of the 'push' of a battery, conductors, resistance, series and parallel circuits were all gradually introduced in qualitative ways, and explained and discussed. For a brief summary of the main concepts covered see Table 2. The goal of this part of the course was not only for the teachers to develop competence in wiring up simple circuits, but also, and more importantly, for them to acquire a deeper understanding of the scientific concepts involved.

In addition the teachers were introduced to the range of preconceptions which research has shown that children and teachers hold about electricity and circuits. They were invited to compare these ideas with the ideas they, themselves, held before they started the INSET and to discuss any other ideas about electricity they had encountered in children.

This part of the course concluded with a self-evaluation questionnaire which enabled the teachers to assess their understanding of the ideas they had met.

Table 2	A summary of the basic concepts covered in the inservice course

An electric circuit is a complete (unbroken) pathway.

Electricity is made up of electrons.

Electrons are very, very tiny particles.

An electric current consists of a flow of electrons.

Electrons are part of all atoms which make up all substances.

The electrons are in the wires all the time.

Conductors have 'free' electrons which can move.

The battery provides the 'push' to move the electrons.

The battery voltage is a measure of the push.

A chemical reaction in the battery creates an electric field which produces the push.

All the electrons move instantaneously.

The size of the current in a circuit depends on the resistance.

A series circuit has all the components in a line. There is only one pathway.

The current is the same all around a series circuit.

In a series circuit adding more bulbs increases the resistance and decreases the current. The bulbs

are dimmer and equally dim.

A parallel circuit has branches. There is more than one pathway.

Identical bulbs in parallel are as bright as one bulb alone. The current in each branch is the same.

The current in the battery leads is the sum of the currents in the separate branches.

In a bulb, moving electrons collide with fixed atoms in the filament causing them to vibrate.

The vibrating atoms emit light and 'heat'.

For a detailed account of these concepts written for primary school teachers see Summers, Kruger and Mant (1995) *Current Understanding: electricity concepts and practice for primary and non-specialist secondary teacher education.*

Part 2 introduced further components such as resistors, buzzers, motors and a number of different switches. The basic concepts of electricity and simple circuits from Part 1 were reinforced and extended with the use of this new equipment. The teachers were introduced to the distinction between science and technology, and to the idea that in technology the goal is using electricity and circuits to perform useful tasks whereas science is concerned with explanation for its own sake. Participants were presented with a number of projects which involved designing and making an appropriate circuit. For example one of the projects was to design and make a hamster security alarm - an alarm had to sound if the class hamster escaped.

Part 3 turned to the teaching of electricity. The teachers were introduced to the notion that different types of knowledge are used by teachers and the distinction was made between subject knowledge and teaching knowledge. The nature of science and science teaching was discussed together with possible ways of planning and implementing lessons on electricity.

In preparation for the rest of the research project the latter half of day 3 was devoted to setting conceptual objectives for lessons. Some approaches to devising conceptual objectives were explored and the teachers began the task of considering what aspects of electricity they were going to teach and the concepts they hoped their children would learn.

THE APPROACH OF THE INSET

There were several key approaches used during the training which supported and reinforced each other. The notable ones are described below.

Confidence building

The teachers started the training unsure of themselves and lacking in confidence in their ability to teach electricity. One of the major aims of the INSET was to boost that confidence. It was therefore important that the approaches used reflected this. Group forming and ice-breaking activities were used at the start of each day in order to create a relaxed atmosphere in which the teachers would feel comfortable, both physically and mentally, so that the learning took place in a sociable and enjoyable environment. Day 1 started with an activity in which the teachers anonymously wrote down their 'hopes' and 'fears' for the course. These were read out, again anonymously, to the whole group and individuals realised that they were not alone in hoping for 'greater confidence and understanding in teaching of electricity', or fearing that 'I won't be able to do it'.

Activities

The emphasis of the training was on developing understanding. In order to achieve this the course leaders devised active experiences for the teachers: both practically active or 'hands-on,' and intellectually active or 'minds on'.

The teachers were led through a range of practical activities and introduced to suitable equipment. This increased their practical competence and confidence, widened their direct experiences of electrical phenomena, and allowed them to ask and answer questions which developed their deeper understanding of electricity and the appropriate scientific explanations for that which they observed and experienced.

Throughout the course, as new concepts were introduced, the teachers participated in discussion activities, either in small groups, pairs or in the whole group. Stimulating and challenging questions were constantly posed by the course leaders (the research team) and the teachers were always invited to raise their own questions or problems. Throughout, the intention was to create an atmosphere in which minds were actively engaged.

At the end of each day the teachers were brought together in a circle and asked to share their reflections on the day and relate one thing they had learnt which had particularly impressed them. This activity had several functions. It aimed to involve the teachers in actively consolidating the day's learning as well as emphasising the group support and confidence building. Some of the comments made at the end of day 3 were as follows:

> the way concepts overlap - to understand one you need lots of other subordinate concepts.

> knowing how to put it over to kids - sorting out the details of what is to be done and then starting at the right place.

> assumptions (I made in the past) about the previous knowledge of kids.

Similarly, at the start of days 2 and 3 the participants sat in a circle and, in turn, were asked to share the most significant thing that they could remember from the previous week. This activity not only served as an ice-breaker and engaged the group's attention, but also provided a means to recap, and focus on, the previous week's learning.

Understanding

A significant feature of the explanations offered during the course was the use of analogies and models. A range of analogies and models was used to introduce and explain several of the electrical concepts. A particularly helpful analogy was a bicycle chain for a simple circuit (see Chapter 3). Here the bicycle chain represents the electric circuit, the moving links in the chain represent the moving electrons which constitute the electric current, and the push on the pedals represents the push on the electrons provided by the battery. All the models and analogies linked things or events with which the teachers were familiar to the new electrical concepts that they were learning.

SIGNIFICANT LEARNING ACHIEVED

It was evident from both the comments made during the sessions and the responses to the feedback questionnaire that significant learning had taken place.

When the teachers were asked to name the most important things about electricity and circuits they had learned from the course the following were the most frequently mentioned:

> an electric current consists of a flow of electrons.

the battery provides a push to move the electrons.

the electrons all move instantaneously.

the current in a circuit depends on the resistance.

When asked to explain what had helped them learn these things all of the teachers mentioned the bicycle chain analogy. In addition the following were mentioned by more than one teacher:

making the circuits and measuring the current with an ammeter.

the use of all analogies and models.

all concepts were carefully and thoroughly explained.

the success of connecting up things to make them work and relating to real life examples.

When asked in what ways they thought their teaching would change as a result of the course, the following were the main features of the responses:

I will ask (and answer) more challenging questions of the children.

I will have increased confidence in subject knowledge.

I will concentrate more on children's understanding.

I can provide more challenging activities and projects.

I will be able to use lots of useful analogies.

When asked to name any ideas they held before the course which they now realised were **misconceptions** the following responses were most frequently given:

the electrons move fast around a circuit.

some electricity (or current) is used up in a light bulb.

the battery is the source of the electrons.

voltage and current are the same thing.

18

SIGNIFICANT DIFFICULTIES

A significant difficulty was encountered on day 3 when the teachers were introduced to the notion of conceptual objectives. They were clearly unfamiliar with the technique of planning lessons by first setting such objectives. They felt uncomfortable with this and did not know where to start. As the aim of the research project was to investigate developments in children's understanding of electrical concepts it was important that the teachers were able to specify the concepts they hoped their children would learn.

However, as soon as a possible alternative approach was suggested many of the teachers noticeably relaxed and focused upon it. This alternative approach was to start with a practical project, for example, wiring up a burglar alarm for a model house. With the project as the end point, the teachers could then work out what concepts the children would need to understand in order to complete the project. They could then decide what concepts they would need to teach and so set conceptual objectives for the lessons. Most of the teachers felt more familiar with this 'project first' approach. Some, though not all, of the teachers did start their lesson planning from this perspective. See the case studies in chapters 3 to 5.

CONFIDENCE AFTER TRAINING

At the end of the training a positive rapport had built up amongst the teachers and between the teachers and the research team. They were enthusiastic about their new knowledge and looking forward to trying it out in their classrooms. They were reassured that they would have ongoing support from the research team. They were noticeably more confident and this was reflected in the feedback questionnaire in which they were asked to rate, again on a scale of 1 to 5, how confident they now felt about teaching electricity. All of the teachers increased their rating by two points, as compared with how they rated their confidence before the training. The teachers who had scored 1 (little confidence) before training now scored 3. Those who had scored 2 before training now scored 4.

SUMMARY

This chapter has described the training course in which the teachers participated at the start of the project. Training was necessary to develop the teachers' subject knowledge and teaching knowledge. The course was over three days and covered the basic ideas and concepts of electricity and simple circuits, an introduction to some new components, and the teaching of electricity. Confidence building, active learning and the development of conceptual understanding were key features of the INSET. Significant learning took place and the teachers finished the training with increased confidence and prepared for the next stage of the project.

CHAPTER 3

JOAN: A LINGUIST TEACHES ELECTRICITY

> ### PROLOGUE: summary of scientific knowledge used in this case study
>
> *Circuit*
>
> A circuit must form a complete pathway for an electrical device to work. It can be series (in line) or parallel (branching). Parallel is better because bulbs are brighter when in parallel than when in series. Circuits can be represented by circuit diagrams using symbols.
>
> *Electric current and electrons*
>
> An electric current consists of electrons, already present in the circuit, moving in one direction.
>
> *Battery and volts*
>
> The battery provides the push for the electrons to move. The size of the push is measured in volts.
>
> *Conductors and insulators*
>
> Conductors allow an electric current to be present. Insulators do not.

ABOUT JOAN

Joan was a junior/secondary trained certificated teacher who began her career teaching French for 4 years to secondary children. After an absence of a few years to start a family, she had returned to teach French as a part-time specialist in an 8-12 rural middle school (deemed primary). Joan was now in her 5th year as a full-time class teacher of 28 Year 7 children in that school and, as such, was expected to teach all curriculum subjects.

In her own schooling she had studied physics and chemistry to the age of 14 and biology to 16. She could not recall any science forming part of her teacher training course. Although comfortable with her knowledge of biological science she confessed that before taking part in the research, electricity was an aspect of science she asked colleagues to teach to her class.

BEFORE TEACHING

Joan's objectives and the children's learning
The INSET Joan received as part of this research focused on concepts and on a pedagogy which stressed the importance of taking into account children's *existing ideas* about electricity.

The prologue above reflects Joan's nine objectives i.e. the ideas she wanted her Year 7 children to acquire. Each child's understanding of an idea before and after teaching was investigated by the research team and expressed on a scale ranging from 0 (little or no understanding) to 2 (good understanding). Substantial changes in children's mean scores (Table 3) showed that Joan's teaching of the group was *very* effective.

Table 3   Joan's 6 children - changes in the group's understanding

TEACHER'S OBJECTIVES Children should understand that:	CHILDREN'S MEAN SCORE	
	Pre-teaching	Post-teaching
1. an electric circuit is a *pathway* which must be complete for a current to be present.	2	2
2. an electric current consists of *electrons* moving in one direction.	0	1.5
3. the electrons are moved by a push which is provided by the battery.	0	2
4. the size of the push is indicated by voltage.	0.33	2
5. some substances, *conductors*, allow an electric current to be present (e.g. water) - others, *insulators*, do not.	1	1.33
6. with some devices (e.g. buzzers), if the connections to the battery are changed round, they do not work - i.e. they are 'one-way' *conductors*.	0.17	1.83
7. there are two ways of connecting components: in *series* (in line) and in *parallel* (branching circuit).	0.67	2
8. in *parallel is better* because bulbs are brighter than when in series (when connected to the same battery).	0.17	1.67
9. real-life circuits can be represented by *circuit diagrams* with symbols acting for components.	0.83	1.83

KEY: 0 = little or no understanding   2 = good understanding (max. score)

Joan's planning

During the INSET Joan had met two possible ways to plan a teaching sequence:

- first choose a set of ideas about electricity she would wish the children to learn and then devise experiences which would enable this.
- select a practical project for the children to undertake and then consider the ideas they would need to master in order to do this.

Joan opted for the second approach since a major influence on her planning was the desire to engage the children's interest and motivate them. The project chosen was to build a device, described in the INSET materials, which indicates when it is raining ('a wet playtime warning system'). This was very appropriate since her children supervised other classes during wet play times and were often unsure if a play time was designated 'wet' or not. Her objectives expressed the ideas she thought they would need in order to build the device.

Joan's choice of a project approach was also influenced by her uncertainty about the children's capabilities and the problem of knowing where her learners were starting from. Early on, she worried about how much guidance she should give in designing the device although the children did later create their own ingenious designs independently (Fig 5).

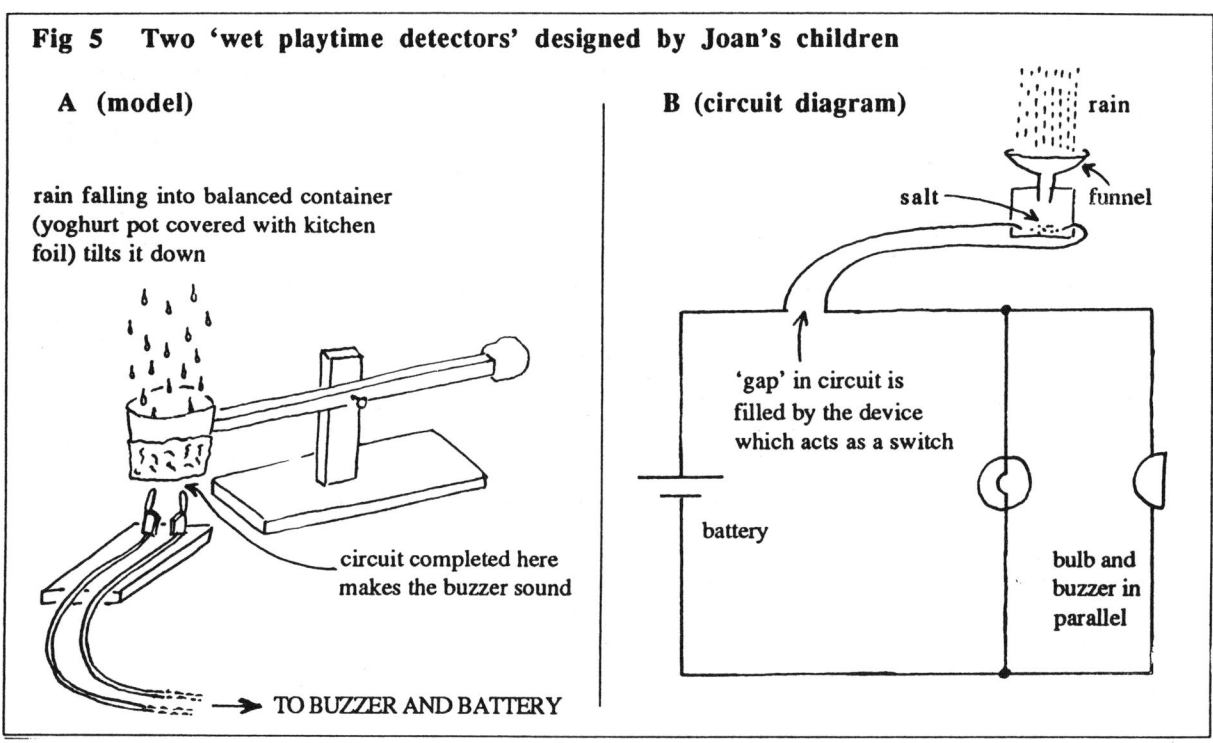

Fig 5   Two 'wet playtime detectors' designed by Joan's children

A (model)

rain falling into balanced container
(yoghurt pot covered with kitchen
foil) tilts it down

circuit completed here
makes the buzzer sound

→ TO BUZZER AND BATTERY

B (circuit diagram)

rain

salt — funnel

'gap' in circuit is
filled by the device
which acts as a switch

battery

bulb and
buzzer in
parallel

Joan initially found it difficult to plan her electricity teaching with conceptual objectives in mind, but she had experienced planning 'backwards' from an end product to objectives when teaching technology.

> Teacher: I must say that when we were first asked to come up with objectives for what we were going to teach, I was really flummoxed. I thought, 'I've no idea!' because I found it so difficult that I didn't know what they (i.e. *the children*) knew, so I didn't know what to start from. So the idea of having a project and going backwards from that seemed an ideal way of coping with it.

She realised that to teach in this way, her own conceptual understanding needed to be adequate:

> Interviewer: How did you used to teach compared to now, after the INSET?
> Teacher: I would never have delved into their understanding of what actually happens in a circuit - just that they understood that a circuit was necessary for a bulb to light would have been the objective.
> Interviewer: You would have stopped there?
> Teacher: Yes and *I* never understood. *I* had this consumption belief *(see later)* before going on the course!

Her focus on concepts was influenced by her knowledge of children's ideas gained from the INSET but was also strongly affected by overhearing the researcher interviewing children about their ideas (see Fig 6):

> Teacher: I heard you talking to the children .. about what was happening in the wires .. (they had) some fantastic ideas of lights flashing and I thought about that. I had never even thought, wasn't really interested, about what was happening because it never occurred to me what electricity was.

Fig 6   Situation used by the researchers to investigate children's ideas about what is happening in a simple circuit

Julie is looking at different parts of the circuit on the table. Imagine that she is wearing 'X-ray mega-magnifying superspecs' which let her see what is happening <u>deep inside</u> things.

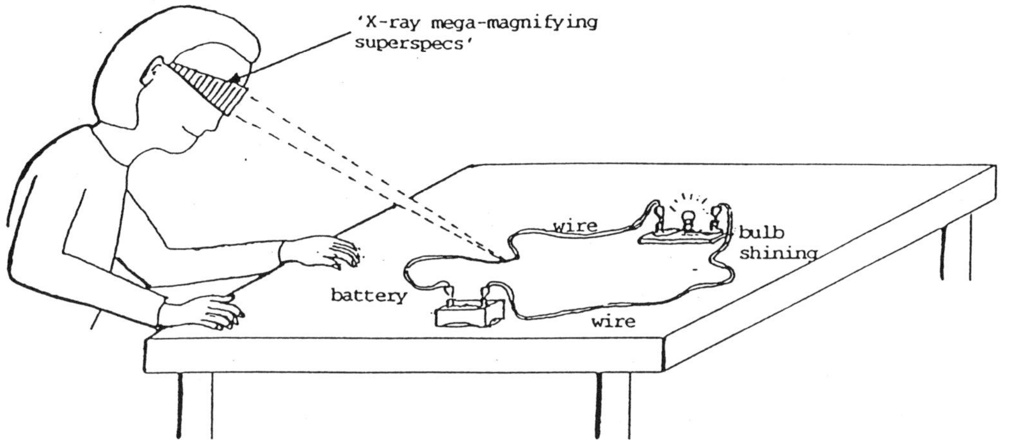

'X-ray mega-magnifying superspecs'

wire

bulb shining

battery

wire

Write what you think Julie would see happening ...   1. ... inside the wire
2. ... inside the bulb
3. ... inside the battery

Joan planned thoroughly and diligently. She gave much thought to sequencing of ideas, use of language and the questions she would ask, and used written notes to guide her through the sessions. During planning, her confidence see-sawed:

Teacher: Sometimes I understand about parallel circuits, sometimes I don't, and I only need a child to ask a question in a different way or to make a comment and I'm thinking, 'Oh, is that right or not?'

Joan realised that:

• some of her objectives required a deeper understanding than she had first thought.
• her own understanding of some ideas to be taught was uncertain and 'ephemeral'.
• discussion with children might lead her into areas she felt were beyond her competence.

So an important constraint on Joan's planning was her confidence in her own understanding. She used her judgment to limit her objectives to those she felt comfortable with. Discussion with the researchers helped Joan to clarify some of her own ideas and, when necessary, recast objectives into a simpler, more limited form e.g. teaching simply that parallel circuits are 'better' than series ones (without explaining this in terms of current).

At first Joan worried that she should be able to address any issue that children raised but later accepted that it was legitimate to restrict children to chosen objectives by using a postponement strategy for difficult points that arose.

Timing was another factor affecting Joan's planning. As she developed her plans, objectives which she felt to be too demanding in the lesson time available were discarded:

Teacher: *'A bulb's brightness indicates the amount of current'* is an objective I've scrapped because it was too much and I don't think it's necessary for them to achieve the aims and complete the project.

It is interesting that Joan planned solely from the materials she had used during INSET, in contrast to her normal practice which was to use as wide a range of sources as possible:

Teacher: I haven't actually looked in any other resources - I've used what we were given on the course.

Interviewer: Normally you would range around and look at other resources would you?

Teacher: It's the only alternative - I collect as many books as I can find, use what I can and go from there.

It is evident that in some aspects of planning Joan still needed guidance and reassurance from an 'expert', despite intensive training which had put her in a better position perhaps than most other primary teachers. She felt that, with no science specialist on the staff (in contrast to an increasing number of other local middle schools), she needed continuing contact with an 'expert' after training to reinforce her new knowledge.

Such a person could also provide the help Joan needed with her technological 'know-how' of equipment (e.g. when to use 6 volt or 1.5 volt batteries). These technological problems showed Joan the importance of trying out activities to ensure that they would 'work' before giving them to children. She did take equipment home to practise with before teaching but still had difficulty coping with some situations that arose in the classroom.

THE TEACHING

Overview of teaching sequence

Joan decided to teach 4 one-hour sessions over four successive days to a group of 3 boys and 3 girls who represented the spread of ability in the class. These were respectively described by Joan as 'very bright boy', 'able, quiet and knowledgeable scientifically', 'below average - least able of the 3 boys', 'brightest girl in the class', 'quite confident - average ability', 'below average - least able of the group'. Joan deliberately excluded the most scientifically knowledgeable child in her class because 'he might question me too far'.

Joan's class was lively and demanding so, in view of the pressures she was under from the demands of the research and to maximise her interaction with this group, she used a technology area adjacent to her room, while a colleague took the rest of the class. This 'ideal' situation was not that dissimilar from her normal practice of teaching groups and it did enable the research to focus on those aspects of Joan's teaching which were of interest, without interference from the effect of, for example, class management problems.

The main focus and content of each session are summarised below.

• *Session 1* *- the circuit as a complete pathway; role of the battery voltage; electrons (objectives 1 to 4)*	Children assembled a simple circuit and described its workings. Ideas about electricity, current, the battery and voltage were introduced in terms of electrons. Children applied these to their own ideas about the circuit which were then investigated e.g by using a current meter. An analogy was introduced to explain the scientific view of what happens.
• *Session 2* *- conductors and insulators (objectives 5 and 6)*	Children tested various materials to see if they were conductors (e.g. water which, owing to anomalous results, was retested at the start of Session 3 using a 6 volt battery). Children's ideas were further investigated and discussed, particularly those about the *direction* of movement of electrons in circuits. Devices whose working depends on this direction (e.g. buzzer) were introduced.
• *Session 3* *- series ('in line') and parallel ('branching') circuits (objectives 7 and 8)*	Children were taught how to assemble the two types of circuits and compared their effects on the two bulbs used and with a single-bulb circuit (also briefly repeated in Session 4).
• *Session 4* *- a project (building a device to detect when it starts raining)*	In pairs, the designing of a 'wet playtime detector', which had begun in Session 3, was completed. The device was built (with references back to various ideas from Sessions 1-3 when difficulties arose) and then tested and evaluated.

In Session 1 circuit diagrams were introduced as a means of representing the real-life circuits being built and these were developed throughout the rest of the sessions (*Objective 9*). During Sessions 1-3 Joan explained to the children the use of unfamiliar items of equipment when necessary. Safety issues were dealt with at the start of Session 1 and repeated in Session 4.

How did Joan achieve her objectives?
Enabling children to grasp the ideas she had chosen as objectives made demands on two types of knowledge which Joan possessed:

- her own personal understanding of these concepts (*subject knowledge*).
- her knowledge of ways in which to make the ideas accessible to learners (subject-specific *teaching knowledge*).

We can look at Joan's use of these two types of knowledge more closely by examining in detail how she dealt with some of her objectives when teaching. The excerpt below, from Session 1 audio/video transcripts, shows the coherent sequence in which Joan taught objectives 1-4. As will be seen, when she first introduced objective 2 it was with reference to a small portion of wire. She revisited this later to expand the idea expressed in the objective to the entire circuit.

OBJECTIVE 1 - AN ELECTRIC CIRCUIT IS A PATHWAY WHICH MUST BE COMPLETE FOR A CURRENT TO BE PRESENT

Joan's subject knowledge

Joan knew the scientific view that electricity consists of tiny particles called electrons, and when these electrons (the electricity) move in one direction along a wire they form an electric current. Although she used the term 'current' very occasionally in her speech or visual aids, she usually referred to 'electrons' or 'electricity' when teaching. This point is discussed in more detail later. Joan also possessed the idea of a circuit as a complete pathway, which superficially seems fairly straightforward. However, during the INSET Joan had been introduced to details of children's views about the nature of this pathway and was aware that they often held non-scientific views (Fig 7). Indeed her own view had formerly been a 'consumption model' in which 'electricity' is used up (consumed) by the bulb (Fig 7b). Her subject knowledge of the nature of the electrical pathway had been changed by the INSET and she now equated electricity with electrons and held the scientific view that the current is the same all around the circuit.

Fig 7   Children's views about the nature of the electric circuit as a pathway

a. 'Source-sink' model	b. 'Consumption' model	c. 'Clashing currents' model	d. Scientist's model
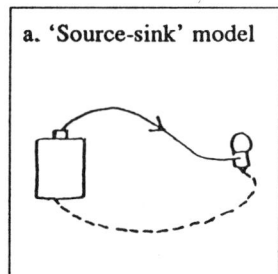	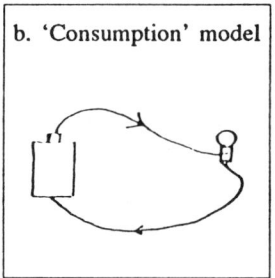	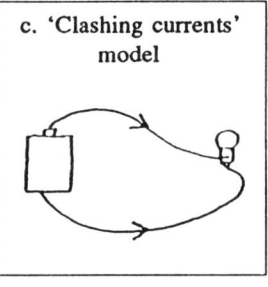	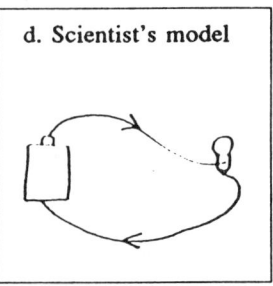
current from battery to bulb - only 1 wire needed	*more current in 'outgoing' wire than in 'return' wire*	*current comes from each end of battery to the bulb*	*same current in one direction around circuit*

What Joan did with the children (teaching knowledge)

Joan knew from her training that an awareness of children's existing views was an important aspect of teaching knowledge. Overhearing some of her children's ideas when they were interviewed by the researchers added to her resolve to use elicitation of their views as a key element of her approach. In Session 1 Joan gave the children the task of making a bulb light in a simple circuit to see if they understood the need for the circuit to be complete (which they all did). She then asked the children for their ideas about what was happening to the 'electricity' in the circuit:

Teacher:	There has to be a complete circuit for that bulb to light but what is actually happening in these components .. the wire .. the bulb .. the battery?
Darren:	.. electricity coming out of the battery and .. into the bulb.
Teacher:	What is electricity? What do you think it looks like?
Lyn:	Wavy lines.
Neil:	Sparks, clusters of white sparks going .. into the metal bits .. of the bulb
Laura:	I don't think you can see it.

She took care to ensure that the route of the pathway inside the bulb- and battery-holders was understood by carefully pointing out the connections made to the bulb and battery inside them. From these initial children's ideas Joan moved on to another of her objectives:

OBJECTIVE 2 - AN ELECTRIC CURRENT CONSISTS OF ELECTRONS MOVING IN ONE DIRECTION

Joan's subject knowledge
This 'sub-microscopic' view of the nature of an electric current, in terms of a flow of electrons, had been acquired by Joan during the INSET provided earlier in the research programme.

What Joan did with the children (teaching knowledge)
Using a visual aid on a flip chart (Fig 8), she presented to the children, as an alternative to their own explanations, the scientist's view that 'electricity' consists of electrons (already present in the wires) and an electric current is these electrons moving in one direction:

Teacher: *(points to first drawing)*
There you've got a piece of wire - this is a bird's eye view of it. What scientists believe is that electricity is made up of very tiny, tiny particles .. so minute you can't see them .. called electrons in the wire and all the components .. jiggling about .. not going in any direction. - in there all the time, whether there is a flow or not.
(turns to second drawing)
When the circuit's complete .. there is an electric current running through the wires, these electrons are made to move in one direction.

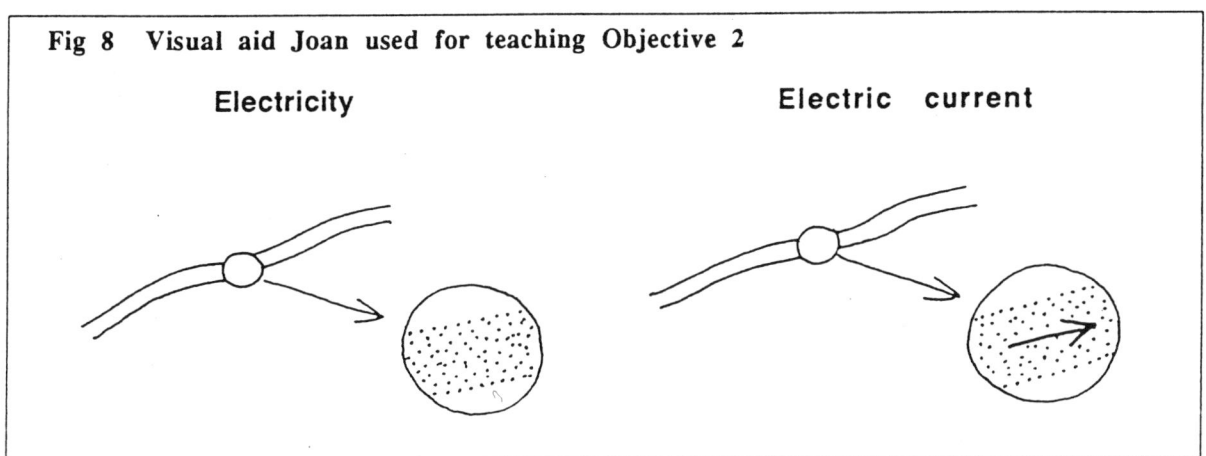

Fig 8   Visual aid Joan used for teaching Objective 2

Electricity   Electric current

The question of what made the electrons move was Joan's next objective.

OBJECTIVE 3 - THE PUSH TO MOVE THE ELECTRONS IS PROVIDED BY THE BATTERY

Joan's subject knowledge
During her INSET Joan had met the scientific view that when the circuit is connected, the battery establishes an *electric field* which exerts an *instantaneous* force on the electrons *all round the circuit* and sets them in motion to form a current.

What Joan did with the children (teaching knowledge)
Joan judged it sufficient merely to present the battery to children as a 'pusher of electrons':

Teacher: What do you think might help them (electrons) move around the wire? ..
Darren: Metal .. because metal conducts electricity
Neil: All the little electrons coming out of the battery and pushing them along.
Teacher: .. scientists believe the battery itself provides the push .. at home it might be a wall socket ..

Joan's next objective was to give meaning to the 'lots of different numbers' that she knew the children must have noticed printed on the casings of batteries.

OBJECTIVE 4 - THE SIZE OF THE (BATTERY'S) PUSH IS INDICATED BY VOLTAGE

Joan's subject knowledge
During her INSET, Joan had learnt that a battery's voltage indicates the amount of push it exerts on any electrons which are within the electric field which the battery produces.

What Joan did with the children (teaching knowledge)
Children were given an assortment of different batteries and asked to examine them (Fig 9):

Teacher: If the battery provides the push - *(she gives out batteries to the children)* - there are different
             types of batteries and they have lots of different numbers on them. Do you know how the push
             is measured?
Neil: In voltage?
Teacher: That's right. Can you guess what the abbreviation might be? What's the size of the push of
             that one?
Lyn: One and a half volts.

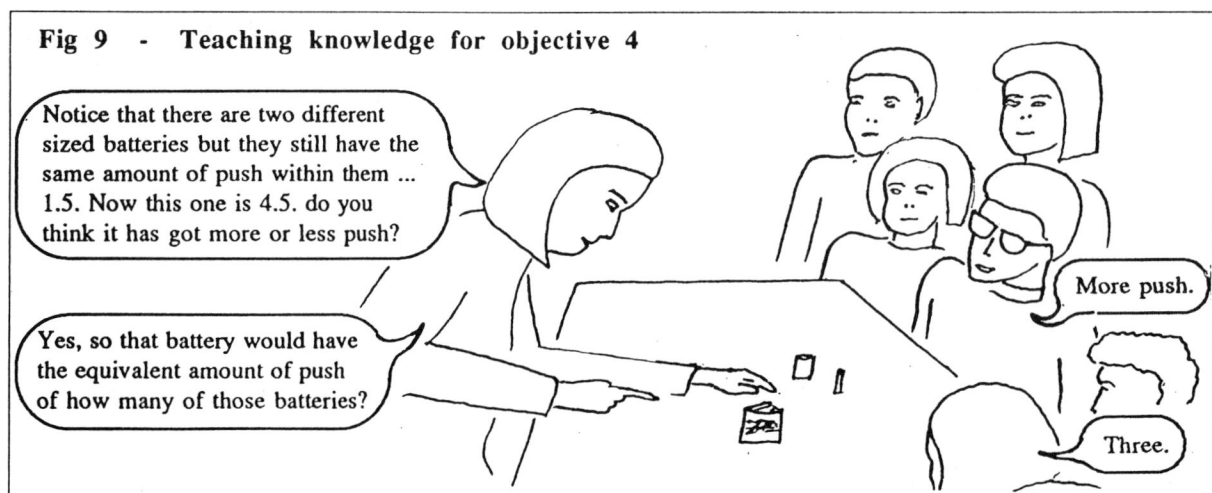

Fig 9 - Teaching knowledge for objective 4

Notice that there are two different sized batteries but they still have the same amount of push within them ... 1.5. Now this one is 4.5. do you think it has got more or less push?

Yes, so that battery would have the equivalent amount of push of how many of those batteries?

More push.

Three.

In her initial treatment of Objective 2 (above), Joan had focused on a small segment of wire. She now returned to this objective and shifted the children's attention to the direction of the electrons in the circuit *as a whole*.

OBJECTIVE 2 (revisited) - AN ELECTRIC CURRENT CONSISTS OF ELECTRONS MOVING IN ONE DIRECTION

Joan's subject knowledge
At the time of teaching Joan firmly held the scientific view that there is the same amount of current all round a circuit. Her previously held 'consumption' view of electricity in a simple circuit (Fig 7b) had been disproved by using a current-measuring meter, called an ammeter, during INSET. This had been a notable experience for her which, as will be seen, she passed on to her children.

What Joan did with the children (teaching knowledge)
Joan asked the children to explain their ideas about what is happening in the whole circuit in terms of 'pushed electrons'. Children revealed a range of ideas about what was happening which underpinned their apparent understanding of the need for a circuit to be complete, shown at the start of the session. Below Joan is suggesting that Helen expresses her view about what is happening in the whole circuit in terms of the battery pushing electrons, an idea that she has introduced to her. Helen explains that she thinks the electrons go along just one of the wires only as far as the bulb (see Fig 7a):

Teacher:	Where do you think the electrons go when the bulb is lit? (Children: Mm ..) Why not suggest that the battery is pushing the electrons .. where to?
Helen:	Into the bulb .. (the electrons go) up into the bulb .. and then they turn to light.
Teacher:	And you think it stops there? *(Helen nods)* Right.

This hypothesis was quickly rejected by the children, on logical grounds, when Joan reminded them that *two* wires were needed for the circuit to work:

Teacher:	You don't need this wire then do you? What happens if you take it off?
Darren:	The light goes out.
Lyn:	It's not a proper circuit - it is not a complete circuit.
Teacher:	So what's that wire there for then?
Laura:	To complete the circuit.
Darren:	The electricity goes to the battery.

Next another hypothesis was advanced:

Darren:	It goes down one (wire), up there (into bulb) and goes back down the other (wire to the battery).
Jack:	Yes and then when it gets less powerful it could go round again ...
Laura:	(Electrons) come out of one end of the battery, to the bulb and go back when they're not as powerful and go through the battery to get charged up again.

29

Here the children think that the electrons are 'less powerful' after passing through the bulb and that they are 'charged up' again by the battery. This belief resembles the scientific view according to which the electrons are the means by which energy is transferred from the battery to the bulb (the electrons are not themselves used up in this process). However, Joan interprets these responses (probably mistakenly) as a belief that current is used up (the consumption model of Fig 7b), and asks the children to investigate this consumption idea by providing them with current-measuring meters (called ammeters) to 'measure the amount of electricity in the wires' (Fig 10):

Fig 10   Investigating the 'consumption' model (extracts from taped dialogue)

Showing 'sameness' like this all round the circuit did not affect one child's belief about *direction* - Neil still firmly believed the electrons travelled *from each end* of the battery and met in the bulb:

Neil:	i think the electrons get pushed to the bulb - they go up there and .. burn up to make light.
Teacher:	From where do you think?
Neil:	Both wires - they go up there and burn to make light.

Joan postponed investigation of this 'clashing currents' idea (Fig 7c) until the next session, although with more knowledge and exploration of the meter, she could have introduced the idea that the device indicates current *direction* as well as size:

Teacher:	Has that (using the meter) changed your opinion?
Neil:	Um - I think it's still the same.
Teacher:	.. you think it (the meter) will show the same anyway because it's the same amount of push from either side (of the battery)?
Neil:	Yes.
Teacher:	Well I'll not talk about that any more until tomorrow because that needs more equipment.

30

[In the next session, Joan introduced devices (e.g. a buzzer) which only allow electrons to pass through them in one direction. Use of these convinced Neil of the scientific view that the electrons' direction was *towards* the bulb on one side and *away from it* in the other (Fig 7d).]

An effective analogy

Joan now transferred into the classroom from her INSET some teaching knowledge which she as a learner had found effective. She moved over to an upturned bicycle placed on a table and used it (Fig 11) to reinforce and develop several of the ideas she had introduced so far:

- the battery as a 'pusher' of electrons

Teacher:	This is called an analogy, it's a sort of comparison. You know how a bicycle chain works? An electric circuit works the same. The pedals are the push on the bike chain. What's the push in an electric circuit?
Lyn:	The battery.
Teacher:	So the pedals are the battery.

Fig 11   The bicycle chain analogy - Joan's visual aid

Bicycle chain   **Electric current**

- the electrons (already in the wire) all start moving at the same time

Teacher:	What might be the links?
Jack:	The wire.
Teacher:	What's inside the wire?
Jack:	Electrons.
Teacher:	So - when you push the pedals the chain will start moving .. all of these links .. start moving together. When the battery provides the push, the circuit is connected, that will start to move the electrons around and they all start moving at the same time .. What could this (rear wheel) be if we are comparing it with an electric circuit?
Darren:	The bulb.

- the electrons move in the same direction all round the circuit

Teacher:	If (the chain) is very similar (to the circuit), what direction do you think the electrons move in?
Neil:	One way.
Helen:	.. (but) I haven't changed (my mind). I think they (the electrons) are different going round ..

after they have passed into the battery, new ones come out.

Teacher: Why? Do you suddenly get different links on the chain (after the pedal has turned)? Do you get new ones there?

Jack: (*pause*) They are the same.

- the strength of a battery is a measure of its 'push'

Jack: If the battery runs out, the electrons stay still ...

Teacher: (Yes) when the battery wears out is like when your legs get tired and you can't pedal any more.

Joan concluded the work on these objectives by getting the children to make drawings of the bicycle chain and the analogous circuit.

Summary

Subject and teaching knowledge used by Joan in the effective sequence described above is summarised in Table 4.

Table 4   Some subject and teaching knowledge used by Joan in Session 1

SUBJECT KNOWLEDGE	TEACHING KNOWLEDGE
The electric circuit forms a complete *continuous* pathway.	Show the children how bulb holders and battery holders work i.e. how connections inside them link to the sockets which connect to the wires.
Electricity consists of electrons.	(1) Bicycle chain analogy: links = electrons. (2) Visual aid: electrons, always present, 'jiggling' in the wire move in one direction when battery is connected.
An electric current consists of moving electrons.	Visual aid, as in (2) above (see Fig 8) and the bicycle chain.
The battery pushes electrons that are already there in the wire.	Bicycle chain analogy: links = electrons pedals = battery.
The size of the push depends on the voltage of the battery.	Discussion of different sort of batteries and the meaning of 'V' on them e.g. 4.5 V has 3 times the push of a 1.5 V battery.
Electric current is not 'used up'.	Investigate size of current at points around the circuit using a current-measuring meter (ammeter). Bicycle chain analogy.
Electric current does not 'converge' on the bulb from each end of the battery i.e. it has a one-way direction around the circuit.	Investigate direction of current at points around the circuit using directional devices (e.g. buzzer). Bicycle chain analogy.
Scientific view of a simple circuit: current is in one direction only and is the same all around the circuit.	Elicit the children's views about what the electricity does in a simple circuit. Use the above strategies to test these views.
Real-life circuits are shown by diagrams with symbols acting for components.	(1) Show the symbols for the components used. (2) Get children to match drawings of real-life circuits with their respective circuit diagrams.

Further examples of subject and teacher knowledge used by Joan in other sessions are shown in Table 5.

Table 5   Other subject and teaching knowledge used by Joan (Sessions 2 and 3)

SUBJECT KNOWLEDGE	TEACHING KNOWLEDGE
Salt water is a good conductor. *Note:* This is more evident with a 6 volt battery than with a 1.5 volt one. If a suitable buzzer is used to indicate conduction, rather than a bulb, tap water can be shown to be a conductor.	Get the children to: (1) place this and other substances across a gap in a circuit *containing a buzzer*. (2) build a 'wet playtime detector' in which drops of salt water make a connection across a gap in the circuit.
A parallel circuit is 'better' than a series circuit because bulbs shine more brightly when in parallel than when in series.	Get the children to: (1) light 2 bulbs in series and in parallel. (2) observe the brightness of the bulbs each time.
When two bulbs are connected together in parallel, there are really two separate, independent circuits. When in series, the two bulbs are part of the same circuit.	Get the children to: (1) light 2 bulbs in a series circuit and then in a parallel circuit. (2) observe and explain the effect of unscrewing one of the bulbs in each circuit.
A buzzer is a 'one-way' conductor of electricity.	Get the children to: (1) make a buzzer work, noticing its connections to the battery. (2) reverse the connections and explain what happens.

COMMENTARY

The teaching described above was clearly *effective* according to the criteria used in this research i.e. the children did acquire the ideas expressed in Joan's objectives (Table 3). This success is a considerable achievement for a non-specialist teacher who was teaching these ideas, only recently acquired by herself, for the first time.

Planning

A key feature of Joan's planning was the way she used strategies to limit her teaching to concepts with which she felt comfortable. This involved setting the right (for her) objectives, and recognising that she could legitimately stick to these and avoid being led into more difficult areas. Joan's use of a 'theory before practice' approach helped her here:

Teacher: I'm happier doing the theory first because then I'm happier that they understand properly .. this way I've got more control over the theory that I give them .. my subject knowledge is, I feel, so poor that .. I could give the children an experiment they have got to deduce things from and they may well have deduced things that I can't cope with and don't truly understand myself. So in this way I have got control ..

Interviewer: And that control gives you more confidence obviously, because you can eliminate things in the subject matter that you are unsure of?

Teacher: Yes.

This pragmatic decision allowed her to maximise her control over the content that was likely to arise during a session.

Of course, the implication of such an approach is that a teacher has to know the appropriate theory to present. Joan did use *presentation* as a key part of her teaching. Children were not expected to induce scientific ideas from activities (an extremely unlikely outcome). Hence, although for Joan the approach had a pragmatic and protective purpose, at a more philosophical level it effectively ruled out naive inductivism (the notion that children will somehow *discover* for themselves ideas generated by some of the greatest minds which have ever lived).

Subject knowledge

The subject matter knowledge shown in Tables 4 and 5 was used confidently by Joan and reflected accurately the ideas she had been taught in the earlier INSET course. However, there were ideas linked to her objectives which were dealt with less certainly.

- Joan taught (incorrectly) that the electrons moved from the positive terminal of the battery to the negative one. All teachers found difficulty with electron movement and current direction during the INSET programme. In Appendix VII we revisit these ideas and describe a new analogy which may be helpful.

- The use of an ammeter was not dealt with clearly by Joan, and children were not clear about what it was measuring (see Chapter 6). Joan did not realise that an ammeter can be used not only to measure the size of the current, but also indicates the direction. Use of the meter to indicate direction could have been a valuable strategy in helping to refute the 'clashing currents' misconception held strongly by one of the children (see page 30). At a cost of about £5, an ammeter is a valuable tool for refuting this common misconception.

- Apparently simple activities using electrical apparatus can give rise to technical problems which, if practical solutions are to be found, require deeper subject knowledge than that which is being taught e.g. when to use 6 volt rather than 1.5 volt batteries (many buzzers require 6 volts), or why both a buzzer and a bulb fail to work when in series (needs the concept of resistance). This was a recurrent theme in all three case studies, and is an important issue for primary teachers.

Teaching knowledge

Some of the teaching knowledge used confidently by Joan is shown in Tables 4 and 5. As the elaboration below indicates, most of the knowledge was acquired during the earlier INSET.

- Simplification of ideas to make them accessible to learners is a key aspect of teaching knowledge. The evidence from the INSET, and from the children's learning in this case study, is that certain ideas, not commonly used in primary science, are readily grasped and used confidently by primary teachers and children. These ideas include

- electricity as electrons
- battery as a 'pusher' of electrons
- battery voltage as a measure of the push
- electric current as the consequent flow of electrons.

Of course, in the present instance these simplifications were advocated by the INSET team and simply adopted by Joan. While for Joan they probably represent subject knowledge, for experts they are teaching knowledge.

- The use of a bicycle chain as an analogy for a simple electric circuit had helped Joan's own understanding during INSET and was used very successfully in her teaching. In fact 5 out of the 6 children taught by Joan mentioned this explicitly as something which helped their understanding (see Chapter 6).

- Joan knew from research findings described during her INSET that children are likely to hold particular misconceptions about electric circuits (see Figure 7). In her teaching she deliberately elicited the children's prior conceptions and did indeed find that these misconceptions were present. However, the key point is that she did not just elicit these views for their own inherent interest. She followed them up explicitly and was able to use specific strategies to focus on and refute the children's misconceptions e.g. the bicycle chain analogy and use of a current measuring ammeter to refute the 'consumption of current' model.

- Again from the INSET, Joan had gained experience of using appropriate equipment and setting up circuits to illustrate ideas expressed in her objectives.

- Joan had thought very carefully about language in her planning, and was very aware of the need to use appropriate terminology and clear expression:

Teacher: I know that I'm never precise in the sort of language I use. There were several occasions when I thought I should have used the scientific language. I thought I was using 'electricity' too much and not 'electrons'. Once or twice I thought I was using the wrong vocabulary (or) the wrong noun or whatever. I hope I managed to keep going and didn't confuse the children. I didn't think they appeared to be particularly confused. I suppose they are used to me anyway.

Despite this awareness, there were occasions where Joan's use of language may have produced unintended learning outcomes. For example, perhaps there is a link between

Teacher: When the circuit's complete .. there is an electric current running through the wires, these electrons are made to move in one direction

and the view expressed by one child in a post-teaching interview that

Lyn: Electric current is a current running through the wires making electrons move with the current.

Joan knows very well that the moving electrons *make up* the current, but this was not emphasised in the teaching, and this child (Lyn) seems to have developed the view that current and moving electrons are distinct.

• Knowing what to emphasise is an important part of teaching knowledge. Knowledge of children's common misconceptions is of key importance here, and was a key feature of Joan's teaching. So, for example, while the concept of a circuit as a pathway is a notion which children may readily accept, it is known from research that they may hold a range of non-scientific views about the *nature* of this pathway. Joan was aware of this and emphasised what was happening *within* the pathway in her teaching. Further examples of where emphasis may be needed in teaching are apparent in Chapter 6, where the children's learning is examined in detail.

The consumption model

In her INSET course Joan had been taught that electricity consists of tiny particles called electrons and that when these electrons (the electricity) move in one direction, they form an electric current. In other words, an electric current is made up of moving electrons (moving electricity).

The bicycle chain analogy used by Joan is very useful in helping to convince children that current is not 'used up' (consumed) by the bulb in a simple circuit. In this analogy, the pedals correspond to the battery, the moving links to the moving electrons, and the back cog wheel to the bulb (Fig 12). Clearly, the current (the moving links) is not used up when the bulb lights (the back wheel turns). Joan understood this clearly herself, and rejected correctly the 'consumption of current' model shown in Fig 7b.

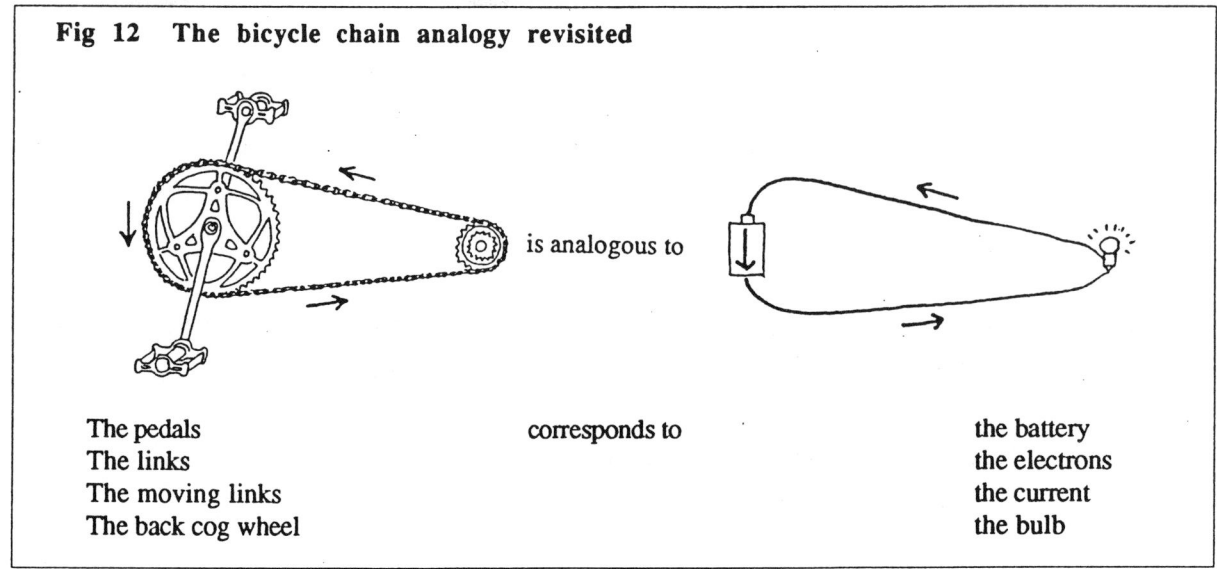

Fig 12   The bicycle chain analogy revisited

is analogous to

	corresponds to	
The pedals		the battery
The links		the electrons
The moving links		the current
The back cog wheel		the bulb

However, as the dialogue at the bottom of page 29 indicates, children cling strongly to the idea that something must be 'used up' if the bulb is to light. This intuitive idea *is* in accord with the scientific view: something is 'consumed', but it is *energy*, not current. The scientific view is that the electrons are the means by which energy is transferred from the battery to the bulb (we might say 'consumed' by the bulb), but they are not used up in the process. Joan does not mention this in her teaching and, although it formed part of the INSET, it is not clear whether she successfully acquired this subject knowledge. Certainly, she did not attempt to use the analogy to explain why the bulb lights and distinguish between energy consumption and current consumption.

This might have been done by emphasising how the moving links push on the back wheel cogs, causing them to move (gain energy). Similarly, in the electric circuit, the moving electrons collide with the fixed atoms in the bulb filament as they are pushed through it, causing these atoms to vibrate vigorously. This vibration is felt by the finger touching the bulb as 'heat', and vigorous vibration of these atoms in the bulb also causes them to emit light.

The bicycle chain analogy for an electric circuit is not the only one which can be used in primary schools. Other possibilities are discussed in Appendix VI, together with a discussion of their strengths and weaknesses.

Chances for development

When reading transcripts of teaching sequences and of the interviews with children, the research team were struck by the number of instances where, with just a little more explicit teaching, children's ideas could have been consolidated or extended, or partial understanding and lingering misconceptions more explicitly addressed and resolved. The team characterised these missed opportunities as 'chances for development'. In some cases, there is no doubt that these missed opportunities were deliberate omissions as a result of conscious pedagogical decisions. However, from our vantage as experienced science educators, they are ideas we would encourage teachers to consider. They are described in the context of children's learning in Chapter 6, under the heading 'Could the teaching have been developed?'.

Some other characteristics of Joan's teaching

- Planning and structure

    This was very thorough. Children were led along a clear developmental path with their final goal being the knowledge needed to construct a rain detector.

- Conceptual focus

    Her concern was to develop children's *ideas* rather than just their skills or factual knowledge. The concepts to be developed were expressed explicitly in her planning and addressed explicitly during teaching.

- Presentation

    Children were not left to induce correct scientific ideas merely from doing activities. Scientific ideas were *presented* didactically in the form 'scientists believe that ...' and suggested as alternatives to the children's ideas.

- Challenge   Joan used specific activities and frequently asked particular questions which were designed to challenge children's thinking.

- Reinforcement She used recaps frequently, at the beginning and end of sessions, and invited children to describe something they had learned at the end of each session (a technique she had met during the INSET sessions).

AFTER TEACHING

Joan's perceptions

After completing the teaching sequence, Joan talked to the research team about:

(1) the success of her teaching in general and in terms of particular objectives.

Joan judged her performance in terms of the children's learning and understanding of 'what was happening' in the circuits, their use of the equipment introduced and familiarisation with it, and their ability to build the rain detector device.

In these areas, she thought the children had achieved the improvement hoped for and she felt that most had acquired the concepts expressed in her objectives. She described how her six children 'really did enjoy taking part' and were 'talking about it ... even after the final session'. Initially she had worried that her aims 'were probably too low' but was vindicated by what she found the children did not understand.

(2) the factors affecting this success.

Joan attributed her success to a hands-on approach, working with individuals, being able to hand-pick the group, the intensity of the teaching (because there were no 'outside influences' to do with monitoring the rest of the class), the 'wonderful' equipment provided, and the use of the bicycle chain analogy.

Joan also mentioned the tight control she exercised on the scope of the sessions as a factor influencing her success. The constraints which caused her to rigidly adhere to her plans were the demands of the research, the ideas she wanted to teach, the limited time available (a major constraint) and her lack of confidence. .

(3) the difficulties she had met.

A further constraint was, of course, the difficulties she had met such as her worries about 'having to delve into "what is a current?" and the idea of the rate of current and speed etc'

38

(she acknowledged her deliberate avoidance of the word 'current' in her teaching). Other difficulties Joan mentioned were problems with equipment, her uncertainty about whether to teach conventional and electron current and her lack of confidence about this idea, her avoidance of the notion of resistance, and worries about how she would respond to questions children might ask about the basic ideas in her objectives. Joan also felt she had difficulty with her lack of knowledge of where the children were (conceptually speaking), restricting the children to the objectives she had chosen, and her 'lack of confidence in the subject'.

(4) what she had learned - the changes she would make.

Joan's reservations about whether her children could design a device in the abstract, using a circuit diagram, and then translate that into reality were borne out with two of them but the others, to her surprise, coped well with this task. If she had to re-teach the sessions Joan said she would make it less intensive - probably a 'half term's project' and include the concept of a switch and the notion of resistance.

(5) the main influence on her teaching.

Joan described how she was normally strongly led by the content of published sources and by the decisions of educational policy makers. Her basic strategy of addressing children's misconceptions was very significantly influenced by her reading of the INSET materials used in the research. She said these

Teacher: ... helped me decide that was something I really ought to do because I hadn't in any way shown, or would know, what the children actually believed. Even though they said it was a circuit, they didn't really believe (it) because they thought it (the electricity) was used up in the bulb. The majority (of the children) had a consumption idea.

This shows that INSET which addresses pedagogy as well as subject knowledge can have a profound effect on a teacher's pedagogical practice, influencing and changing that teacher's approach.

SUMMARY

Overall, this effective teaching was characterised by clear conceptual objectives, some personal confidence in the subject matter expressed in these objectives, planning which incorporated strategies to keep the sessions within the bounds of her subject knowledge and appropriate teaching knowledge.

The teaching knowledge included simplification of concepts for pedagogic purposes, use of an effective analogy, elicitation of children's preconceptions and use of follow-up strategies to develop a more scientific view, use of appropriate equipment, experiments and activities, usually careful use of appropriate language and emphasis on known areas of difficulty (although this could have been further developed).

Other features of Joan's teaching included careful and thorough planning, an explicit focus throughout the teaching on the concepts to be understood, explicit presentation of the scientific view and use of strategies to help children accept this, plenty of challenge and both monitoring and reinforcement of children's learning.

CHAPTER 4

LUCY: 'DIVING IN AT THE DEEP END'

<table>
<tr><td colspan="2">PROLOGUE: summary of scientific knowledge used in this case study</td></tr>
</table>

Circuit

A circuit must form a complete pathway for an electrical device to work. It can be series (in line) or parallel (branching). The branches of a parallel circuit are like separate independent circuits. Circuits can be represented by circuit diagrams using symbols.

Electric current and electrons

An electric current consists of electrons, already present in the circuit, moving in one direction. Its size is determined by the devices in the circuit and can be measured with an ammeter. In a parallel circuit the size of the current in the battery leads increases as more branches are added to the circuit.

ABOUT LUCY

Lucy was a junior trained certificated teacher whose career began in 1963. After three years she left teaching to start a family and in 1974 took up her present post at a Junior and Infant school (with nursery) of about 220 children from a mixed catchment area in a small town. During her time at the school, Lucy had taught all junior age-groups. At the time of the research she was a full-time class teacher of 29 Year 3/4 children, teaching all curriculum subjects and acting as the school's language coordinator.

In her own schooling she had studied general science to the age of 16 and had a biology O-level pass. She could not recall any instruction in science education during her teacher training course. Lucy had received 'quite a lot' of INSET in science, both twilight and whole day(s), during her career but electricity had been dealt with in a technological context so that she 'knew what to do .. (like) making a buggy .. but didn't understand what was happening'.

BEFORE TEACHING

Lucy's objectives and the children's learning

Lucy had taught simple electricity (making a bulb light) to her Year 3 children during the current academic year. However electricity was not part of Year 4 science in the school's 2 year rolling programme which was based on the local education authority scheme. Fortunately, she was able to arrange to teach three sessions of an hour each to a class of 33 Year 6 children who had been taught by the school science coordinator the previous year (only 27 of the children were present throughout all 3 sessions).

While Lucy had never been these children's class teacher she knew them well and had taught them all at some stage during their time in the school. The Year 6 teacher had done some teaching of electricity to the class earlier in the year but it was agreed that she was to observe Lucy's sessions and not take part in any teaching.

Table 6 shows Lucy's six objectives i.e. the 'basic concepts' she thought would give the children 'a different way of thinking about electricity - hopefully a clearer idea of what is going on in the models you'll be wiring up'. Here she is referring to models of things seen at a slate quarry during a school visit to Wales earlier in the year which the Year 6 children were making and to which they would be adding electrical circuits (see Fig 13).

As in the other case studies, each child's understanding of the ideas implicit in the objectives before and after teaching was investigated by the research team, using a pencil and paper test, and expressed on a scale ranging from 0 (little or no understanding) to 2 (good understanding).

Table 6   Lucy's 27 children - changes in their understanding

TEACHER'S OBJECTIVES Children should understand that:	CHILDREN'S MEAN SCORE	
	Pre-teaching	Post-teaching
1. current is a flow of electrons from the battery along the pathway and back to the battery in one direction.	1	1.33
2. flow can be altered by use of resistors, buzzers, bulbs (in series), motors and other devices.	0.63	1.07
3. adding components (bulbs or other things as well) in parallel in a circuit can increase the flow of electrons (i.e. current) from the battery.	0.30	0.44
4. things connected in parallel are like separate circuits each drawing current from the battery.	0.33	0.78
5. ammeters are used to check (i.e. show size of) current.	0.56	1.22
6. it's possible to show all the wires and things in a circuit on paper using lines and symbols (i.e. circuit diagrams).	0.53	1.48

KEY: 0 = little or no understanding   2 = good understanding (max. score)

Two boys and four girls, chosen by the class teacher to represent a spread of ability within the class, were interviewed in detail about their responses to the test before and after teaching. Two of these were characterised by the class teacher as 'bright' and the other four were described as 'average' or 'below average'. The 'bright' children attained level 5 and the others attained level 4 (i.e. national average) in national Science Standard Attainment Tasks later in the year.

The changes in mean scores shown in Table 6, obtained from the results of the written test, indicate that Lucy's teaching of the class was moderately effective for some objectives but was less effective for others.

Lucy's planning
At an early stage in the project, when Lucy realised that participation involved a willingness to teach, for the first time, *ideas* about electricity to Year 6 children, she declared herself quite

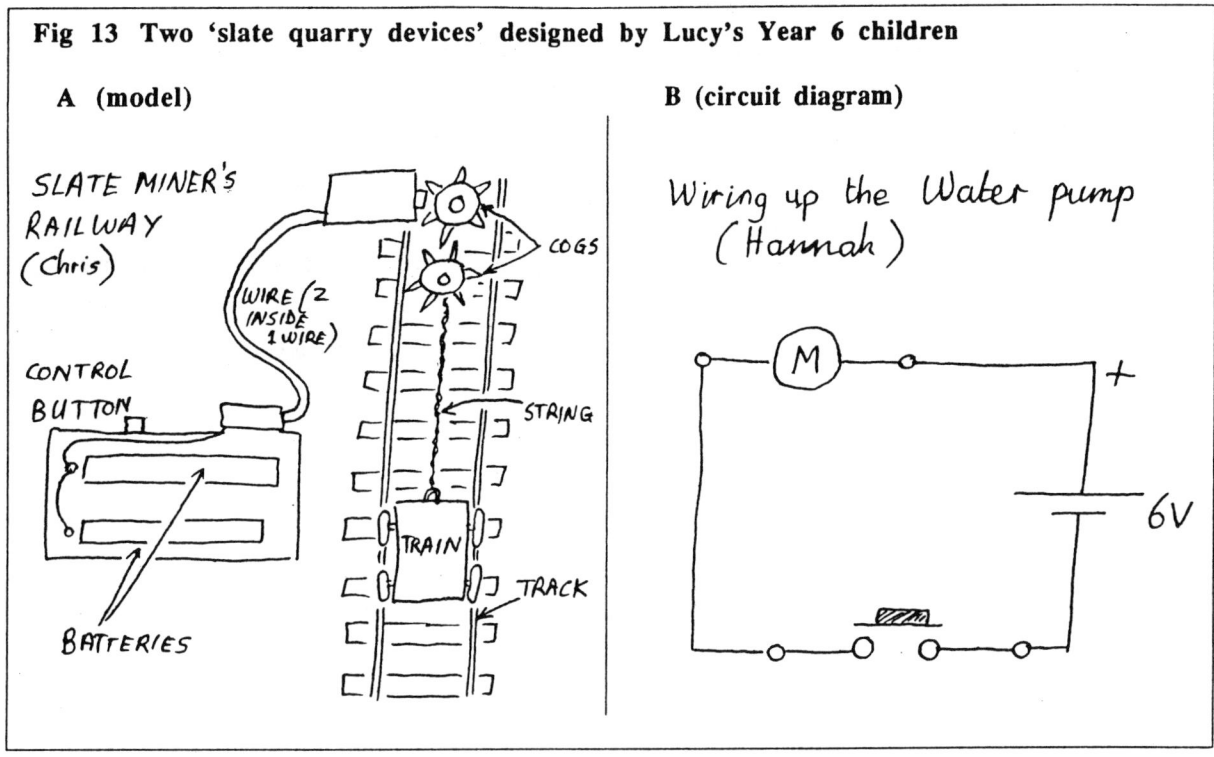

Fig 13 Two 'slate quarry devices' designed by Lucy's Year 6 children

A (model)

B (circuit diagram)

SLATE MINER'S RAILWAY (Chris)

COGS

WIRE (2 INSIDE 1 WIRE)

CONTROL BUTTON

STRING

TRAIN

TRACK

BATTERIES

Wiring up the Water pump (Hannah)

M

+

6V

willing to 'dive in and learn' from the experience. Like Joan (Chapter 3), Lucy had met during the INSET course two possible ways to plan a teaching sequence:

- first choose a set of ideas about electricity she would wish the children to learn and then devise a set of experiences which would enable this.
- select a practical project for the children to undertake and then consider the ideas they would need to master in order to do this.

Lucy used the second approach since a practical project - making models as a follow-up to the children's trip to Wales - was already in progress in the class. She looked through the workshops in the INSET materials 'Current Understanding' which described how to make various lighting and warning devices and 'picked out particular items that I thought would fit'. She examined a list of the concepts covered in the pack (supplied during the INSET) and chose those which

- 'had been of specific interest' to her.
- she 'fully understood' and felt 'able to teach because I know them myself'.
- could be done within the limited time available.
- were relevant to the devices needed for the models the children were making.

During discussion of her planning with the research team Lucy showed understanding of ideas she had met during the INSET and indicated a desire to teach her children *concepts*:

Teacher: I think the children already know about how to connect up the battery to a bulb to make it light .. they don't need that initial playing around with equipment - what they need is to know that it's the flow of electrons that is causing the bulb to light.

However, when Lucy actually started to plan, her confidence was set back by:

- having to 'sit down and actually think about how I'm going to put it over'.
- concern about 'how the children are going to react - I'd be more confident with my own class'.
- the thought of the presence of another teacher and the researchers in the room.
- worrying about 'being well enough planned to know exactly where I am going from step to step'.
- concern about 'what I'm saying to them (hoping that) I don't get myself in a muddle'.
- worries about her use of correct scientific language, for example, using 'an expression that just comes out naturally that isn't correct'.

Lucy was also concerned about the ideas the children would acquire from her teaching:

Teacher: What I worry about as a primary teacher is misleading children into getting wrong concepts.

Other difficulties she encountered during planning were:

- how to control the pace at which the session proceeds in the limited time available.
- not 'skirting over things on a superficial level without going into the knowledge side - explaining and knowing what is happening' (as opposed to procedural learning - the children 'just being able to do it').
- how to get the children to use correct language and 'the right terms'.

Lucy planned to begin with a 'question and answer session to find out what they already know about electricity .. what they have done before'. She admitted that 'I don't know what their understanding is at all' and explained that 'they may not know at all the difference between a series and parallel circuit' although 'apparently they have done both according to last year's teacher'. She thought that her emphasis would be on understanding what is going on in these circuits whereas her colleague may have simply been concerned with children making the circuits work.

Lucy felt that her planning of this work differed from her normal approach in its greater emphasis on 'input and knowledge':

Teacher: (Before) I might have let them more freely use the equipment .. spend more time just experimenting without giving them the input and knowledge. Perhaps I'm giving them a bit more knowledge this way than they would have had got by just experimenting, but they wouldn't have really known what to say, what's happening.

She seemed to be moving from an *inductive* approach, where children are thought to develop valid scientific ideas just from experimenting, to one where her role is to provide some theoretical knowledge for children to explain their findings.

She felt she now had enhanced subject knowledge about electricity as a result of the practical approach taken in the INSET she had received. This was in contrast to other curriculum areas where 'swotting up' subject knowledge before the lesson was a common practice:

Interviewer: So you're more up front delivering knowledge than normally. With other kinds of teaching would you have that knowledge?

Teacher: I would have mugged it up in a book .. staying one step ahead of the kids .. Science for me is a big sort of unknown territory so (before the INSET) this sort of thing was something I'd really have had to read up on and probably wouldn't really understand .. but because I've done it myself in this practical way with you I now hopefully understand it a bit more .. what is actually going on .. than I would have done if I'd launched in without the (INSET) course.

But there were still areas of uncertainty and she felt the need to consolidate and maintain familiarity with the content she had encountered during the INSET:

Teacher: I've obviously got to keep looking at this and reminding myself .. it's not something that's gone in (to my head) .. things will come back and I'll think, 'Of course, I remember that' .. I read this through and through again .. to make absolutely sure that I am familiar with everything there that I want to tell them.

How Lucy's planning worked out in the classroom will be seen in the next section.

THE TEACHING

Overview of teaching sequence
The main focus and content of each session are summarised below.

• *Session 1* *- series ('in line') circuits;* *a circuit as a pathway with* *moving electrons in it* *(objective 1)*	Uses of electricity, safety issues, equipment used. Making a bulb light. Making a motor work using a cell, 2 switches and wires. Adding a bulb to the circuit in series with the motor. Explaining electric current in terms of electrons, using two analogies (marbles in a jar and the bicycle chain).
• *Session 2* *- parallel ('branching')* *circuits; comparing current* *in series and parallel circuits* *(objectives 2, 3, 4 and 5)*	Demonstrating the reduced brightness of 2 bulbs in series (compared with one alone). Wiring them in parallel to show a way of restoring their brightness. Testing the current in both arrangements using an ammeter. Doing a 'complete pathway' worksheet exercise and introducing the symbols for various components.

• *Session 3*
  - representing real-life
  circuits in symbolic form
  (circuit diagrams)
  (objective 6)
	Teaching more symbols for electrical components. Giving a worksheet exercise asking for predictions of what will happen in circuits shown in symbolic form. Asking children to write down their slate quarry project ideas in the form of circuit diagrams (these circuits were to be built in a later session supervised by the class teacher).

How did Lucy achieve her objectives?

Table 6 shows that Lucy had a measure of success in achieving some of her objectives but less success with others. She was not optimistic about the children's learning following her three sessions. As an experienced and competent teacher looking back on something she had tried for the first time, 'diving in at the deep end' to learn from the experience, her comments about the sessions give some valuable insights into the problems other primary teachers may be likely to face. We describe here some of the objectives in which Lucy achieved success in terms of:

- her own personal understanding of the ideas in her objectives (*subject knowledge*).
- aspects of her teaching, particularly her use of subject-specific *teaching knowledge* (i.e. knowledge of ways in which to make the ideas accessible to learners).
- Lucy's comments, made as she looked back on what happened.
- our own observations about the teaching.

OBJECTIVE 1 - CURRENT IS A FLOW OF ELECTRONS FROM THE CELL ALONG THE PATHWAY AND BACK TO THE CELL IN ONE DIRECTION

Lucy's subject knowledge

Lucy knew the scientific view that an electric current consists of tiny particles called electrons moving in one direction along a wire. She also knew that the electrons which constitute the current are already present in the wire and are not produced by the battery, so the wording of her objective refers to the *direction* of the electrons' movement, not their source.

What Lucy did with the children (teaching knowledge)

Lucy taught this objective in all three sessions. In Session 1, working in six groups, each with their own tray full of a whole range of equipment, the children were asked to connect a battery (or 'cell': the term was introduced) and a bulb (both in holders with sockets) using two wires (terminating in plugs) so that the bulb lit. The equipment was new to them but all managed this and proceeded to the next task which was to make a motor operate. Using two switches, children were next asked to 'see if you can control the motor and the light by putting the switches in .. put the motor and the bulb in a series .. the whole series going round'. After ten minutes four groups had succeeded. One of these explained to the rest how they had set up the equipment and Lucy then helped the two unsuccessful groups. In the final six minutes Lucy addressed the whole class:

Teacher: I want to try and draw this all together for you with a bit of information to try and explain what's happening inside the wires while you're connecting everything up and successfully making the things work.

Holding a long glass jar (representing the wire) half full of marbles horizontally she demonstrated how electrons (the marbles) all start moving at once (by tilting the jar to the vertical) when the circuit is connected (Fig 14):

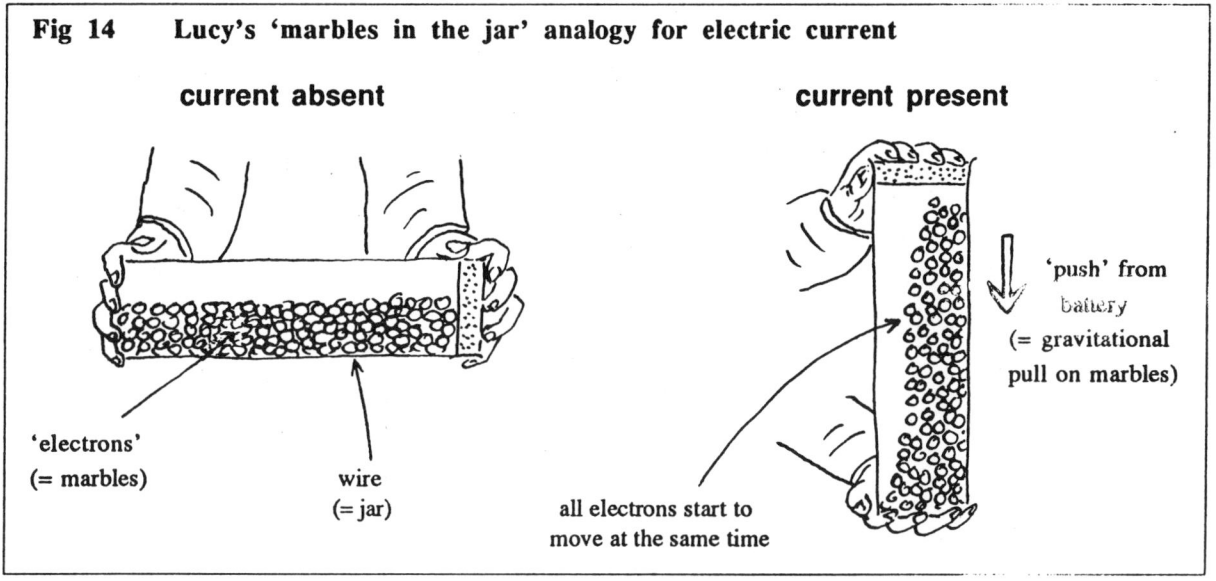

Fig 14   Lucy's 'marbles in the jar' analogy for electric current

current absent   **current present**

'electrons'
(= marbles)   wire
(= jar)

'push' from battery
(= gravitational pull on marbles)

all electrons start to move at the same time

Teacher: I want you to imagine that this is, with your X-ray vision, looking at what's inside the wire of your equipment. Inside the wire are all these electrons - that's what the marbles represent - and when we connect it up correctly in the series, and you've already discovered that you have to connect it all the way round and back to the battery again in order for things to work, there's a push from the battery. A reaction takes place in the battery which starts to make everything move and they all move at once. They don't just push each other along, they all move at the same time (*tilts bottle to vertical*). All those being pushed down to the bottom of the bottle, if you can imagine that those are electrons in there and as soon as the battery gives it a push, they all move at once down the wire .. all at the same time, at the same speed, round the wire.

She also briefly described the bicycle chain analogy before bringing the session to a close:

Teacher: Can you also think about a bicycle? I did think I ought to have asked someone to bring in a bicycle so we could have looked how when you press on the pedals of your bicycle, the whole chain moves at once .. so that it makes the wheels turn. Again that's like the force of the electricity, the force from the battery pushing around and making everything work at the same time. So try and think about what's happening inside the wires of your circuit, what's happening with your battery as you connect everything up.

At the start of the next lesson, Session 2, Lucy revisited the idea of a complete pathway, referring the children to a photocopied diagram in which the following explanation was written in snake-like fashion around the wire's path (Fig 15):

Teacher: (*reads*) 'Electricity must have a pathway to go along. The electric current flows from the battery along the wire to the bulb and then along the other wire back to the battery. Follow this pathway with your finger. We call the pathway a circuit. If any part of the pathway is not joined up, electricity cannot flow right round.'

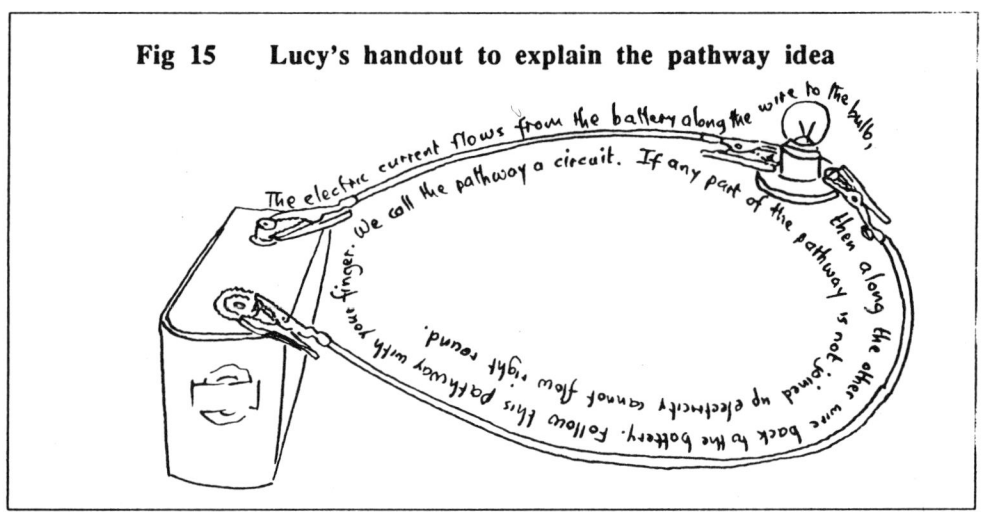

Fig 15   Lucy's handout to explain the pathway idea

Lucy reinforced this in terms of electrons:

Teacher: (If the pathway is not joined up) the flow of electrons won't go right round the circuit. Which children made the single bulb light in their circuit earlier? (*They raise their hands*) Now you know it's very important to make sure you have a pathway for the electrons to be able to flow round the circuit and keep moving and remember I showed you my bottle full of marbles .. as soon as the connections are complete all the electrons start to move at once round the pathway.

Lucy had also referred to the idea of electrons at other times, during Session 1 when talking about the effect of components in a circuit, and again in Session 2 when discussing parallel circuits:

Teacher: All these components act as resistors to the electrons as they are flowing round the circuit .. each time (the electrons) meet one of these resistors it has an effect on the amount of flow of the electrons.

In a parallel circuit you are letting each bulb have an equal amount of the electrons.

Electrons were also mentioned when children were trying to predict what various circuits would do in a worksheet exercise in Session 3:

Teacher: Think back to your pathway. When one bulb (*of 2 in series*) is unscrewed, what will happen? You've got to have your flow of electrons.

Lucy dealt with the notion of a complete pathway for a further ten minutes during Session 2. A photocopied worksheet (Fig 16) showing ways to join a battery and a bulb was distributed. The children's task was a written one - to predict which bulbs will light and explain how to make the other four light. Discussion of answers focused on procedural knowledge, i.e.which part of the bulb or battery the wires should touch, and no reference was made to electrons.

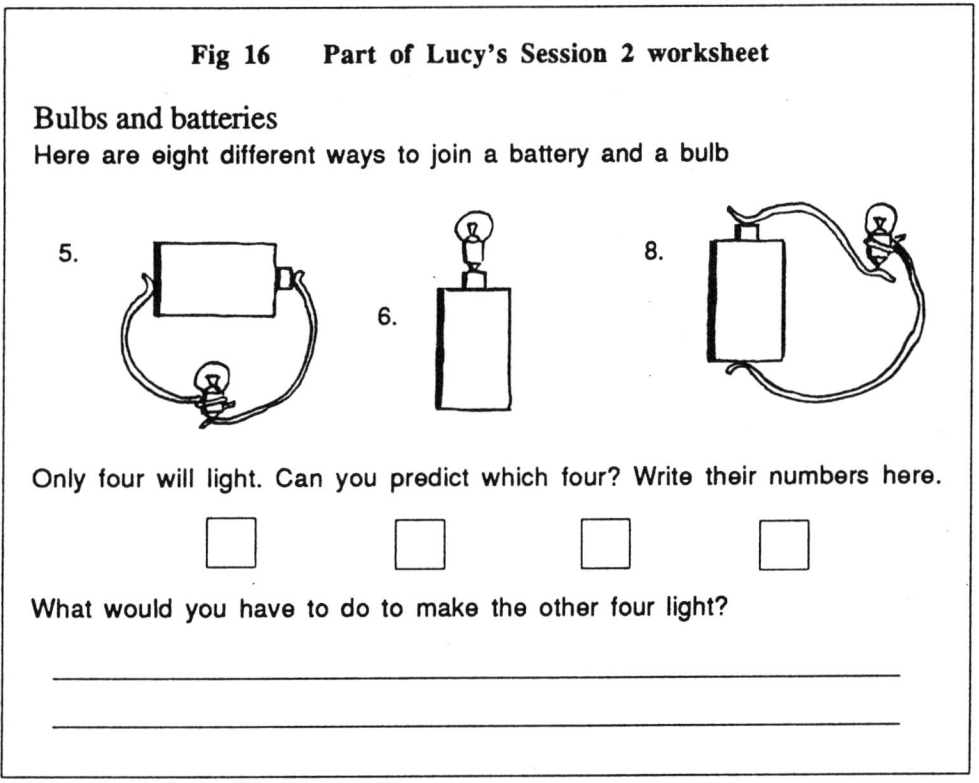

Fig 16   Part of Lucy's Session 2 worksheet

Bulbs and batteries
Here are eight different ways to join a battery and a bulb

5.

6.

8.

Only four will light. Can you predict which four? Write their numbers here.

What would you have to do to make the other four light?

Lucy's comments

Lucy was relieved when the first session was over. She felt that she 'let the children get hands on the equipment too soon' and should perhaps have 'done a bit more theory first'. The session started late and she could have done with 10 minutes more for those who 'hadn't had any success'. She felt that her talk about the analogies was wrongly placed in the session:

Teacher: The marbles in the bottle and the bicycle chain .. was a sort of last minute addition to the
            lesson. It should have been in a slightly more important place.

Lucy felt that the children were excited and 'thrilled to be doing it' and hence she had some problems getting them to stop and listen. She thought that she gave them too many things to put together at once and admitted that she had 'used wrong language here and there' such as 'the push of the electricity around the wires .. the flow of the current' and even as she spoke thought, 'I shouldn't have said that'.

From questioning the children about their worksheet in Session 3 Lucy felt that for most of them Objective 1 had been met.

Researchers' comments

Lucy's relief indicated that she felt under pressure. She did refer to notes while teaching but the shortage of time meant that some of her plans were omitted and others rushed. We agree with her view that the explanations given in terms of analogies should have had a more prominent part in the session. Also, teaching them earlier would have given children the chance to think about subsequent activities in analogical terms. More emphasis could have been given to the bicycle chain analogy since it illustrates so many characteristics of an electric current (see Chapter 3), especially with a concrete example rather than a mere verbal description.

The 'marbles in the bottle' analogy does show well how the electrons all move at once under the influence of an *electrical* field when the circuit is 'switched on'. In the case of the marbles it is the Earth's *gravitational* field that moves them all simultaneously. However, the analogy does not cover other key ideas about current. Pointing out the *limitations* of an analogy to children is perhaps as important teaching knowledge as showing them the correspondences.

Lucy's treatment of these analogies was one-way, from teacher to children, and ways of making the analogies more inter-active might have been tried, such as:

- getting children to explore through questioning and discussion the correspondences between the 'real-life' object and the ideas it illustrates (e.g. if the bike chain is the wire what are the links, the back wheel?).
- letting the children have hands-on experience of the analogy item as well as the electrical equipment.
- asking children to draw and write about the circuit or electrons and their analogical representations.

Lucy directed the activities to some extent and encouraged an investigative approach to the tasks set, but children were distracted by the large variety of electrical equipment presented. Making available *only* those items of equipment required to investigate a particular concept is important teaching knowledge. If this is done, children are more focused, technological problems arising from connecting the wrong components together are avoided, and the teaching of the objective can be consequently more effective (Fig 17).

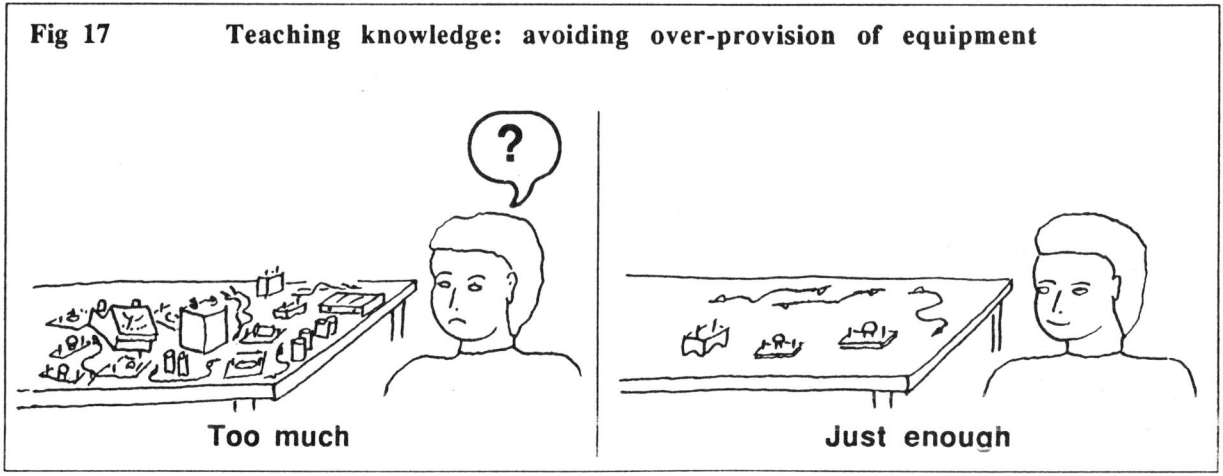

Fig 17   **Teaching knowledge: avoiding over-provision of equipment**

Too much   **Just enough**

The phrases Lucy picked out as 'wrong (scientific) language' showed that she had remembered the rigorous usage encouraged during the INSET. Thus 'the battery pushes *electrons*' is more accurate than 'the force of the electricity' and 'current is *present* (or absent) is preferable to 'current flows' (it is the electrons or electricity which flow). When Lucy used the expression 'in series' the class teacher noticed that this was difficult for some children. Lucy herself was at ease with the meaning of this but had not realised that it needed explanation and more emphasis - perhaps in terms of components being 'in line' or 'one after another like links in a chain'.

An interesting aspect of the language used by Lucy (and probably by many other teachers and published resources) is the misconception implied when she used the phrase 'from the battery to the bulb'. This could give children the impression that the battery is a source of electrons which travel along the wire, which is not the scientific view. Emphasising that 'from battery to bulb' refers only to the electrons' *direction* and that they are *already present* in wires and components is an important aspect of teaching knowledge here.

Data from the written tests show some interesting trends. Before teaching, nearly all children tested already appreciated the need for a complete pathway. When asked to imagine what they would see inside the wire if they wore 'X-ray spectacles', only one child mentioned particles (*'little bits* of electricity rushing round'); of the rest, 17 thought they would see just 'electricity' in the wire. Post-teaching, 9 children mentioned particles in the wire (7 called them electrons).

When asked to define electric *current* pre-teaching, 16 did so in terms of moving 'electricity' or 'power' and 10 either didn't know or referred to 'something'. After teaching, these numbers were 12 and 7 respectively; only 2 children gave definitions in terms of electrons (see Fig 18).

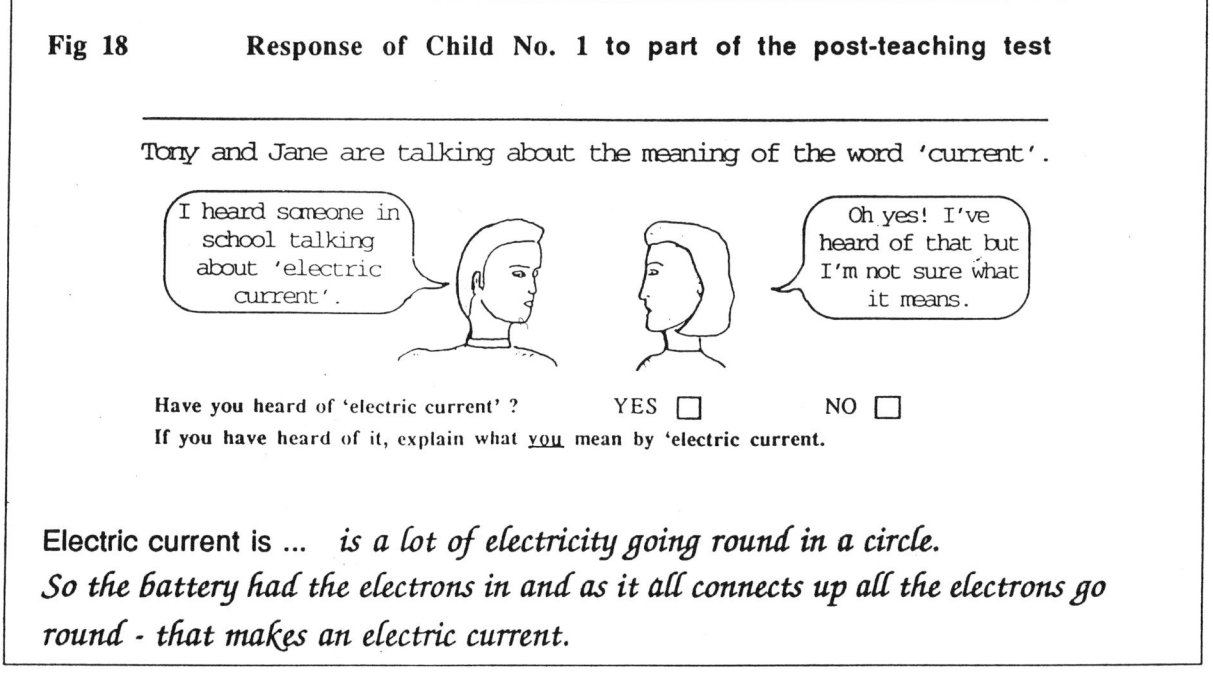

Fig 18   Response of Child No. 1 to part of the post-teaching test

Tony and Jane are talking about the meaning of the word 'current'.

I heard someone in school talking about 'electric current'.

Oh yes! I've heard of that but I'm not sure what it means.

Have you heard of 'electric current' ?   YES ☐   NO ☐
If you have heard of it, explain what you mean by 'electric current.

Electric current is ... *is a lot of electricity going round in a circle.*
So the battery had the electrons in and as it all connects up all the electrons go round - that makes an electric current.

Analysis shows that the pre-teaching score (of 1.00) for Objective 1 indicates the children's understanding of the 'directional pathway' aspect of the objective - none had any knowledge of electrons prior to the lessons. So the emphasis in Lucy's teaching was perhaps too much on an idea that most children already possessed - the notion of a pathway. Time spent on this could have been devoted to dealing with electricity as electrons and the notion of electric current as moving electrons. This might have resulted in a greater proportion of the class grasping these aspects of her first objective.

Lucy did start the first session by asking for the children's ideas:

Teacher:	Can you give me some ideas about what electricity is?
Chris:	A sort of power.
Tom:	It's got so many volts.
Dean:	A force.

However elicitation was limited to this and seemed to be done just for its own sake. It was not used as a starting point for developing children's ideas in the direction of the scientific view. Scientific knowledge was not presented as scientists' beliefs (see Joan's approach, Chapter 3) which are a more powerful and useful alternative to our everyday intuitive ideas.

Lucy's use of material engaged the children in consolidating an idea already present (i.e. the circuit as a pathway) and her handout could perhaps have been used to convey ideas about electrons and current as well (Fig 19).

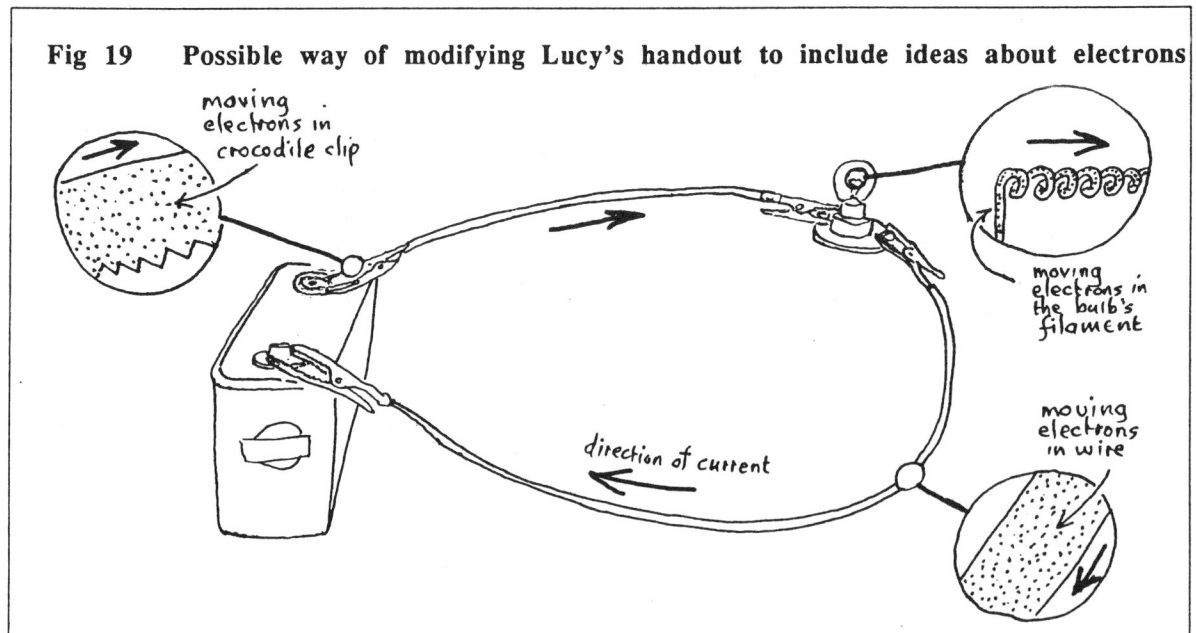

Fig 19   Possible way of modifying Lucy's handout to include ideas about electrons

moving electrons in crocodile clip

moving electrons in the bulb's filament

moving electrons in wire

direction of current

In fairness to Lucy, if this had been her own class she would have had a much clearer idea of where the children were starting from and might have shifted the emphasis of her teaching accordingly. However, her over-optimistic assessment of the children's learning about electrons and current shows:

- the importance of elicitation of children's understanding of specific concepts to effectively 'target' the content of a lesson.
- the difficulty of accurately assessing so many children's understanding during lessons.

It was not surprising that a major insight Lucy had gained from this (for her) step into the unknown was that she would 'never do it with a whole class again' but would teach half the class or preferably, for the purposes of differentiation, small groups.

OBJECTIVE 5 - AMMETERS ARE USED TO CHECK (I.E. SHOW SIZE OF) CURRENT

Lucy's subject knowledge
The INSET had taught Lucy that an ammeter was a 'current-measuring meter'. At first she used the term 'voltage' in this objective but correctly altered it to 'current' when discussing her planning with the research team. Using an ammeter correctly during her INSET and seeing it register a larger current in the lead from the battery each time she added a bulb in parallel to a circuit (Fig 20) had been a memorable event for her.

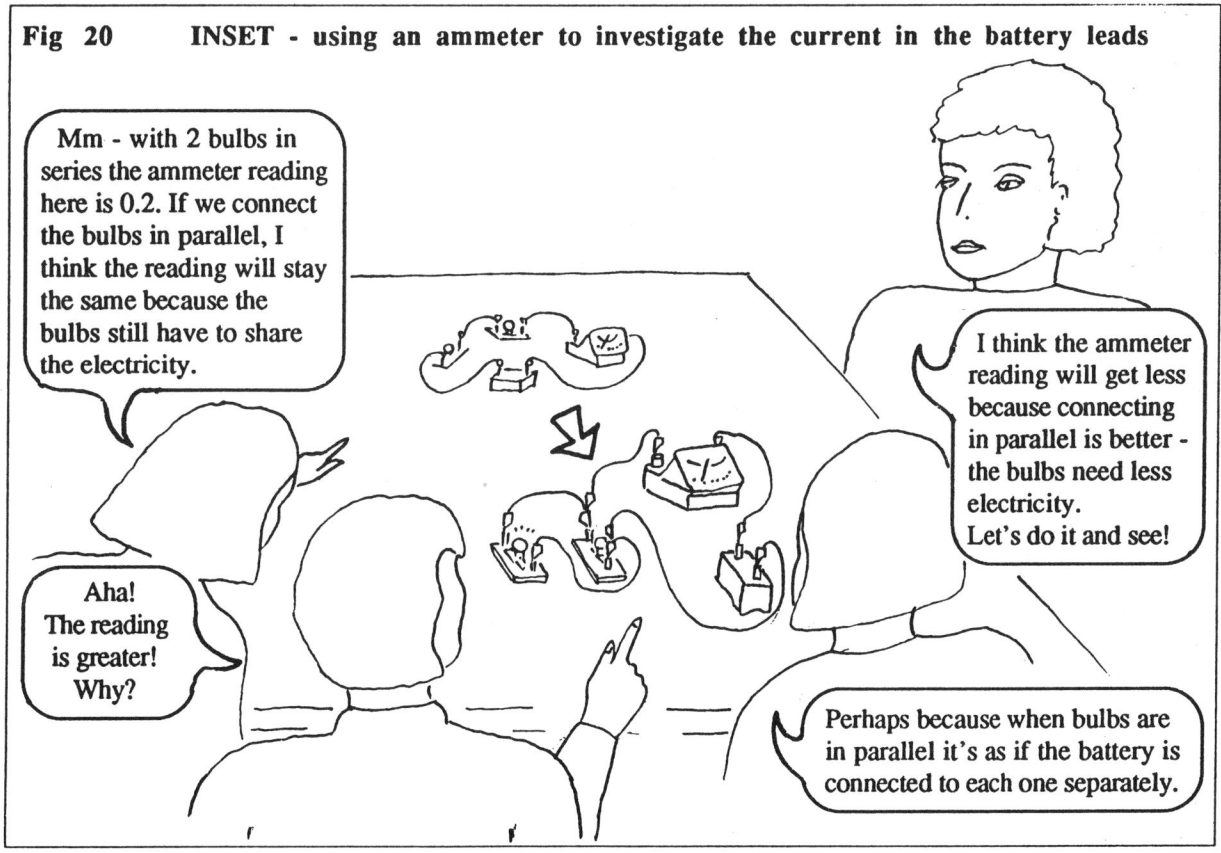

Fig 20   INSET - using an ammeter to investigate the current in the battery leads

Mm - with 2 bulbs in series the ammeter reading here is 0.2. If we connect the bulbs in parallel, I think the reading will stay the same because the bulbs still have to share the electricity.

Aha! The reading is greater! Why?

I think the ammeter reading will get less because connecting in parallel is better - the bulbs need less electricity. Let's do it and see!

Perhaps because when bulbs are in parallel it's as if the battery is connected to each one separately.

What Lucy did with the children (teaching knowledge)
As Lucy described how to connect bulbs in parallel in Session 2, she explained that using the ammeter was a way of testing 'that you are getting more electrons flowing through'. Children were asked to place the ammeter first in a series circuit and 'see what the reading is like'. Next they were to change it to a parallel circuit and then 'test the amount of flow that you are getting

through'. When a child asked how to link the ammeter up in the circuit, the sockets for the leads were shown and the class was told that 'you must make sure that you keep a complete circuit' with 'one lead in one (socket) and one lead in the other'. Children noted the readings on the ammeter as they connected it to many different arrangements of components and batteries.

Lucy's comments

Lucy felt she 'wasn't quite as thrown in the deep end' as in Session 1 and did feel more confident about her subject knowledge in Session 2. However she felt 'not totally secure in what I was saying' and there were moments when she thought 'What's happening? What am I doing .. saying?'. She wanted 'to say nothing rather than give misleading information' but was rewarded by the children's pleasure and interest in the activities.

Lucy's teaching knowledge was tested in this activity. She had difficulty managing the equipment and was puzzled and concerned about the differing ammeter readings the children obtained, particularly the less able. She felt her teaching of this objective was unsuccessful because she hadn't explained how to set up the ammeter and children 'didn't get the ammeters in the correct position on the circuit'. The children 'knew what they were supposed to find but weren't getting the correct reading'. She felt that they were 'picking up on what happened on other tables' and 'probably have some idea but .. I don't think they are understanding'.

Researchers' comments

After the lesson the research team explained to Lucy the anomalous readings which children had obtained. For example, children were not comparing like with like since some used 1.5 volt batteries while others used 6 volt batteries which result in a larger current; many children connected the meter directly across the battery terminals (a 'short circuit') as shown in Fig 21.

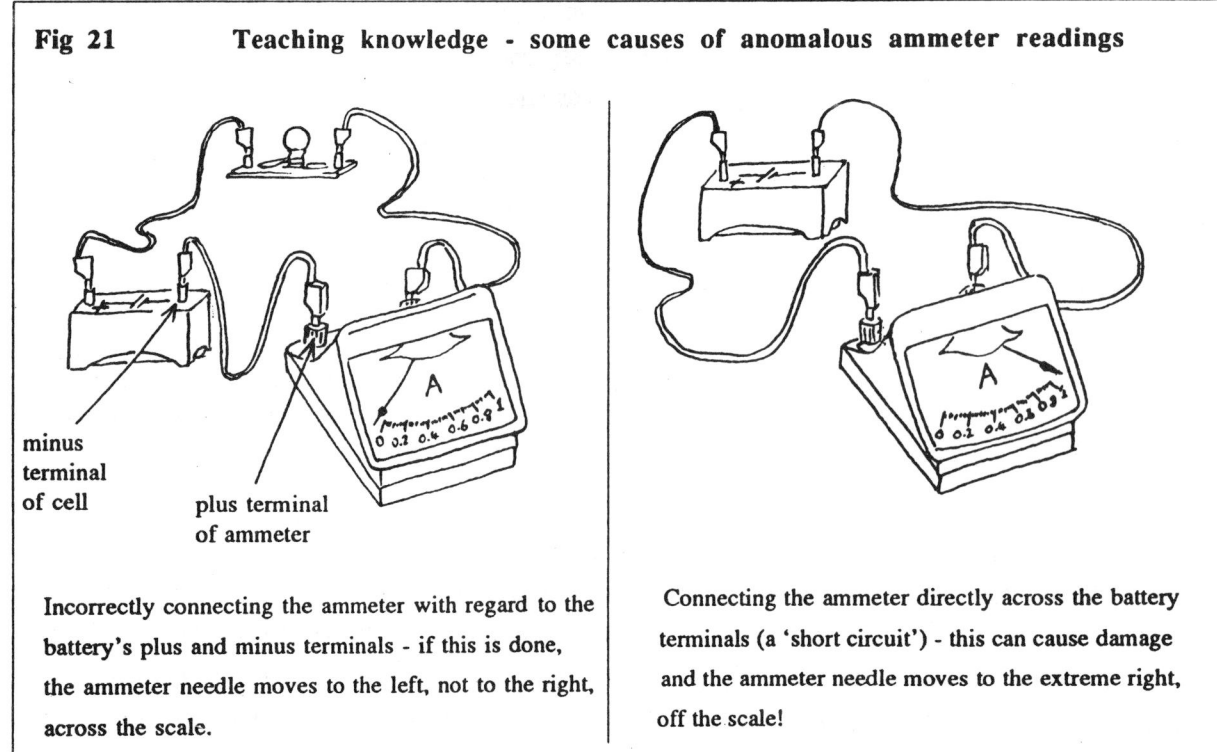

Fig 21   Teaching knowledge - some causes of anomalous ammeter readings

minus terminal of cell

plus terminal of ammeter

Incorrectly connecting the ammeter with regard to the battery's plus and minus terminals - if this is done, the ammeter needle moves to the left, not to the right, across the scale.

Connecting the ammeter directly across the battery terminals (a 'short circuit') - this can cause damage and the ammeter needle moves to the extreme right, off the scale!

So although the INSET had provided Lucy with good procedural subject knowledge - knowing the *correct* way to connect an ammeter into a circuit - it had not explained what happens when it is *incorrectly* connected, which is important teaching knowledge.

For the children, connecting the ammeter was a 'trial and error' activity and Lucy's teaching knowledge did not include giving detailed instructions of how to do this. Of course, even if these are given, children may still misinterpret or ignore them so further teaching knowledge required is knowing the range of causes for unexpected ammeter readings in order that wrong connections can quickly be put right.

Lucy was pessimistic about the effectiveness of her teaching of this objective but a measure of success seemed to have been achieved (see Table 6). Test results showed that before teaching, 6 children thought that an ammeter measured 'current', 'electricity', 'electrons' or 'power' - after teaching 11 did so. So while Lucy's teaching of procedural knowledge (how to connect the ammeter correctly) was not effective, she had taken a few children forward conceptually, closer to the scientific view.

OBJECTIVE 6 - IT'S POSSIBLE TO SHOW ALL THE WIRES AND THINGS IN A CIRCUIT ON PAPER USING LINES AND SYMBOLS (I.E. CIRCUIT DIAGRAMS)

Lucy's subject knowledge
Lucy had learned to recognise the symbols for a range of components during her INSET. She was able to draw real-life circuits in symbolic form and had developed skill with equipment so that she was able to quickly and correctly translate a circuit diagram into an arrangement of wires and components which worked.

What Lucy did with the children (teaching knowledge)
Lucy's teaching knowledge consisted of introducing circuit diagram symbols to the children in a variety of contexts. She used the following strategies:

• give out a handout showing how equipment is represented symbolically.
• name and describe the items of equipment and give children the task of identifying each item (e.g. buzzer, motor, switch) and matching it with its symbol.
• explain the symbols for wires, where wires join (a 'blob'), a bulb, a battery and illustrate on the blackboard how to put them into a circuit diagram.
• explain the correspondence between a real-life circuit and its diagram using the pathway handout (see Fig 15 earlier):

Teacher: .. symbolic diagrams are used by people who are drawing electrical circuits .. (they) are not like the one I gave you first of all (*shows them the handout*) which is just like a picture from real-life (where) you draw the whole battery and whole bulb and put in the crocodile clips and everything. In a symbolic diagram you use the symbols on this sheet (*shows other handout*).

- remind the children that on each item of equipment the symbol was shown:

Teacher: .. you can perhaps see or remember from your little bulb holder (*she demonstrates*) the symbol
              that's usually used to show a bulb in the circuit - a little circle with a wire going through it.

- ask children to interpret numerous circuit diagrams on a photocopied worksheet and
  explain what happens when the switch is operated, a bulb unscrewed etc (Fig 22).

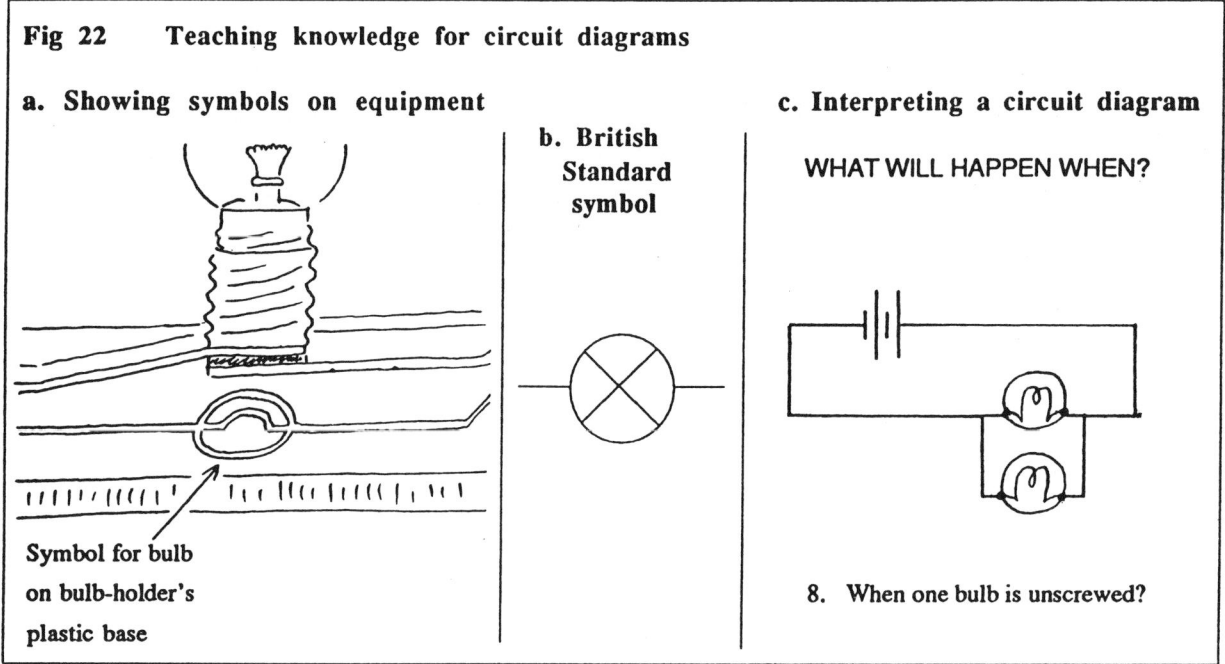

Fig 22   Teaching knowledge for circuit diagrams

a. Showing symbols on equipment

Symbol for bulb
on bulb-holder's
plastic base

**b. British
Standard
symbol**

c. Interpreting a circuit diagram

WHAT WILL HAPPEN WHEN?

8. When one bulb is unscrewed?

Lucy's comments
Lucy thought that the children found this objective 'very hard' and that a major difficulty was
the process of transferring symbols in isolation on a worksheet into a diagram of the whole
circuit. She also felt that children could not move from the real-life representations of their
project models to a purely symbolic representation. It was felt that by introducing so many
different components and their symbols, she had done too much too soon - it would have been
better just to have 'stuck to bulbs'.

Researchers' comments
Lucy seemed quite pessimistic about the effectiveness of her teaching of this objective. Testing
showed that all the children already understood in a general sense that real-life circuits can be
shown symbolically. However Lucy's teaching went beyond this. She improved a number of
children's knowledge of symbols and their ability to interpret circuit diagrams.

Before teaching, only 3 were able to match a real-life example with its correct circuit diagram,
and give reasons for this which involved symbols (Fig 23), whereas after teaching 12 managed
this. So Lucy's teaching knowledge, involving a variety of approaches, seems to have enabled
her to teach beyond her planned objective with some success.

Fig 23   Child No 2's pre-teaching response to the circuit diagram situation in the test

The teacher has asked Zainab to say which diagram on the display board shows how her buggy is connected

Put what you think Zainab says (A, B, C, D, E or F) here _____

DIAGRAMS OF OUR BUGGY CIRCUITS

My buggy's circuit is shown by Diagram ...

Zainab's buggy

Explain why you chose that diagram:
I chose diagram *B* because .. *where the circles are, I think that's the lights. And where the batteries are is the lines on the diagram.*

Lucy's subject knowledge for this objective was good and she seemed comfortable with the demands made of her as she circulated and helped the children. She taught the children a bulb symbol (Fig 22a) which she had learnt from her INSET, and which differs from the British Standard (Fig 22b) but is more intuitive and common in school textbooks. The bulb symbol in the handout she distributed (Fig 22c) was different from both of these.

Necessary teaching knowledge is an awareness of the variation that can occur in symbolic representation of electrical components and a readiness to point this out to children to avoid confusion.

Objectives which Lucy taught less effectively

Table 6 shows that, while Lucy's teaching of Objective 2 seems to have had some effect, that of Objectives 3 and 4 was less effective. This research argues that improvements seen in children's understanding can be attributed to the teaching and this can be analysed in terms of teacher's subject and teaching knowledge. However, reasons for any lack of improvement are less certain since many factors, such as class management problems or children's inattention, could be responsible. However, some observations are offered here.

Lucy's subject knowledge
As a result of the INSET Lucy knew:

- that current varies depending on which devices are placed in a circuit (Objective 2).
- the counter-intuitive fact that the current in the battery leads *increases* as components are added in parallel (Objective 3) - the memorable event shown in Fig 20 above.
- that this increase in current is due to each component, in effect, being in an independent circuit (Objective 4).

What Lucy did with the children (teaching knowledge)
Lucy demonstrated two bulbs in series shining dimly and showed how, if the circuit was rebuilt with only one bulb, that single bulb shone more brightly - the children were asked to explain this. They were then asked to suggest ways in which the 2 bulbs in series could be made to shine more brightly. A child's suggestion that adding an extra battery would do this was accepted but Lucy went on to explain that she 'could do something with just one battery to make the bulbs shine brighter' - by 'adding a lead in a different way' i.e. connecting them in parallel (Fig 24). She then demonstrated how to do this:

Teacher: Instead of joining it round in a pathway like that (*i.e. in series*) I put the leads on as stacking leads and put the bulbs in parallel - I stack the leads like this (*connect the bulbs in parallel*). The bulbs are brighter aren't they? - because this (*the battery*) is performing separately on each bulb .. when you do this you're letting each bulb have an equal amount of electrons from - it's like working as a separate battery, a separate flow of electrons to each bulb. Understand?

Children: No .. Yes .. I'm not sure ..

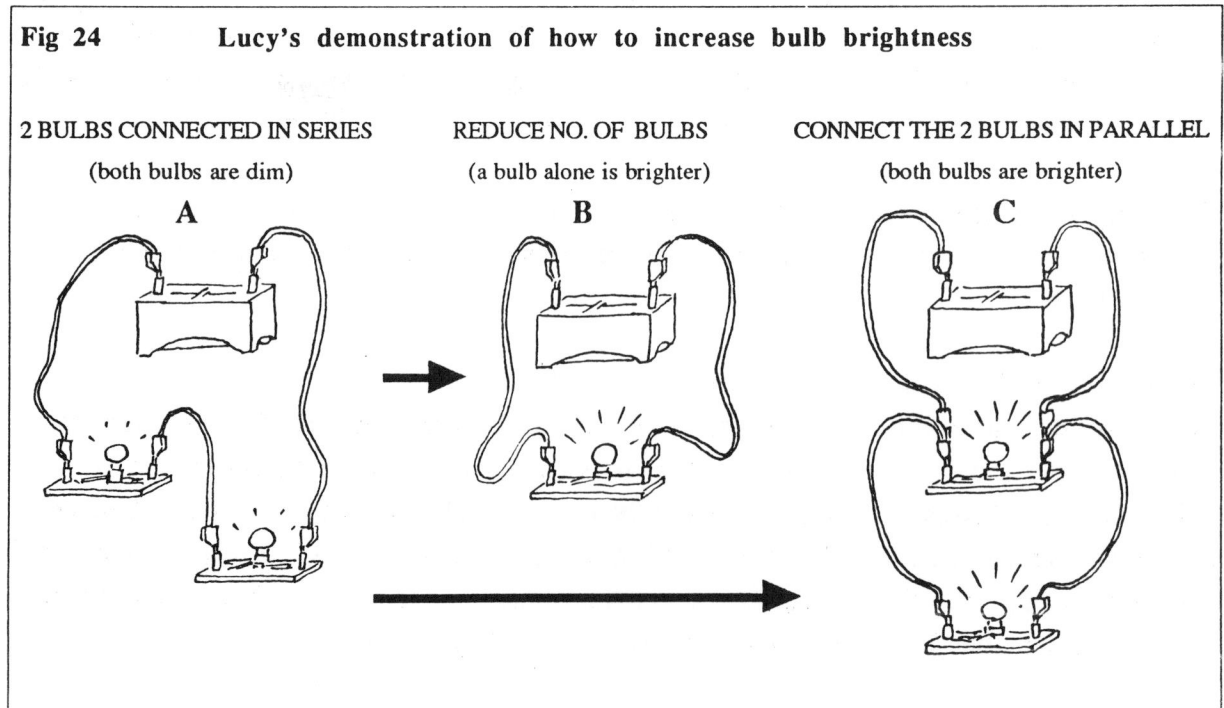

Fig 24   Lucy's demonstration of how to increase bulb brightness

2 BULBS CONNECTED IN SERIES   REDUCE NO. OF BULBS   CONNECT THE 2 BULBS IN PARALLEL

(both bulbs are dim)   (a bulb alone is brighter)   (both bulbs are brighter)

A   B   C

Children were next instructed to try this for themselves:

Teacher: I'll give you your kits and you can see how this works. You can test it, that you are getting
            more electrons through (*when in parallel*), by using your ammeter. Place it first in your series
            circuit and then change it to a parallel circuit, and test the amount of flow you're getting
            through. You should see a difference.
Child: How do you link that (*i.e. the ammeter*) up with it *(the circuit)*?
Teacher: The leads go in here also (*indicates meter sockets*). You must make sure you keep a complete
            circuit. The leads will go into the sockets - some are red and some are black - it doesn't matter.

Some children were absorbed but others became excited as they busily explored various
combinations of other components in addition to the bulbs. As Lucy circulated she reproved
some for 'just messing about' and re-directed them to the task. After 20 minutes, the equipment
was cleared away and children shared their results.

Lucy's comments
Lucy felt the children had understood that the flow of electrons was altered by resistors
(Objective 2) when the resistors consisted of bulbs wired up in parallel, as opposed to in series
(she was non-committal about whether the children understood this with respect to other
components, such as buzzers). She felt this was the case because children had told her they
would do their project in parallel because it would be 'brighter' or 'work better' and also
because children could pick out circuits on the work sheet where this would happen.

She thought that 'most of them' had grasped Objective 3 (that electron flow increases in parallel
circuits) and Objective 4 (how these act like independent circuits) from her demonstration.

Researchers' comments
In planning her teaching Lucy obviously wanted to share some of her greatly improved subject
knowledge with the children. The INSET conveyed these ideas to Lucy with teaching
knowledge consisting of a carefully structured, guided approach making use of explanations
and illustrated analogies with extensive discussion among teachers and course leaders.

The teaching knowledge Lucy used was more limited as, for example, in her explanation of
why two bulbs in series are dimmer than one bulb alone:

Teacher: Can anyone tell me why that should be (i.e. why the single bulb alone is brighter)?
Child: It (the single bulb) doesn't have to share the electricity.
Teacher: That's what people often think, that electricity has to be shared between components. All these
            components act as resistors to the electrons as they are flowing round the circuit .. each time it
            meets one of these resistors it has an effect on the amount of flow of electrons.

Here Lucy fails to stress that 'sharing electricity' is a misconception (in fact the current is reduced by adding a second bulb, so both bulbs shine less brightly). Her alternative explanation is not clear. The children needed to measure the reduced flow of electrons (i.e. current) in the series circuit (2 bulbs) compared with that in the single-bulb circuit. This could then have been explained in terms of a suitable analogy, perhaps like that shown in Fig 25.

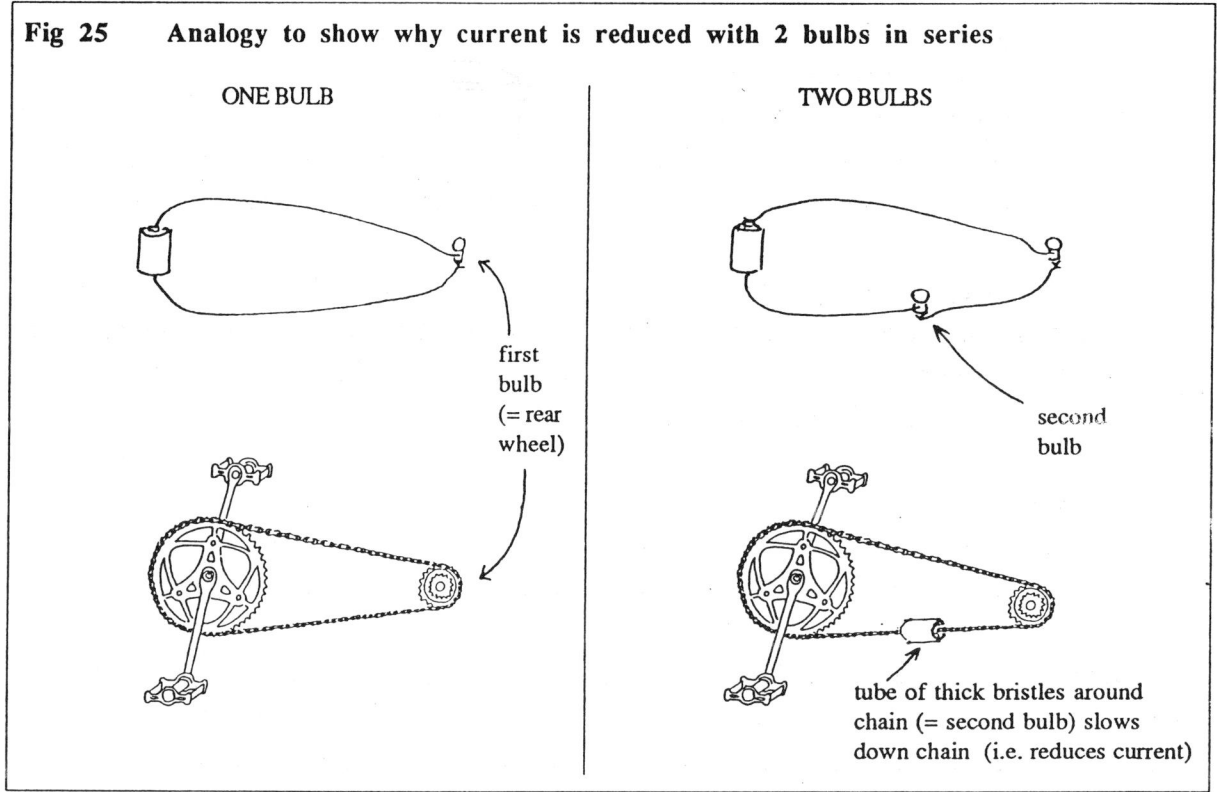

Fig 25   **Analogy to show why current is reduced with 2 bulbs in series**

ONE BULB

TWO BULBS

first
bulb
(= rear
wheel)

second
bulb

tube of thick bristles around
chain (= second bulb) slows
down chain (i.e. reduces current)

When children investigated the size of the current in series and parallel circuits, the hope seemed to be that they would 'find out' through exploratory activity, without too much teacher guidance, the phenomenon that had made such an impression on Lucy during the INSET.

This 'discovery' approach seemed to be borne out in her summing-up:

Teacher: Who can tell me what they've discovered about a series circuit and a parallel circuit? (*children describe their results*). You seem to have different readings on the ammeter - I'm not quite sure why that is - we can investigate it again later.

The wide variation in ammeter readings children obtained, due to the errors discussed above (Fig 21), meant that the session ended unsatisfactorily. Because of this, Lucy was unable to go on to Objective 4 which deals with the reason for the larger current in a parallel circuit.

If the children had been given more precise instructions for the *procedure* of measuring the current, the uniform readings obtained would have enabled her to then move on to the conceptual aspects of the situation, perhaps using teaching knowledge like the analogy shown in Fig 26 as part of an explanation.

Fig 26 Analogy to show how 2 bulbs in parallel behave as if in independent circuits

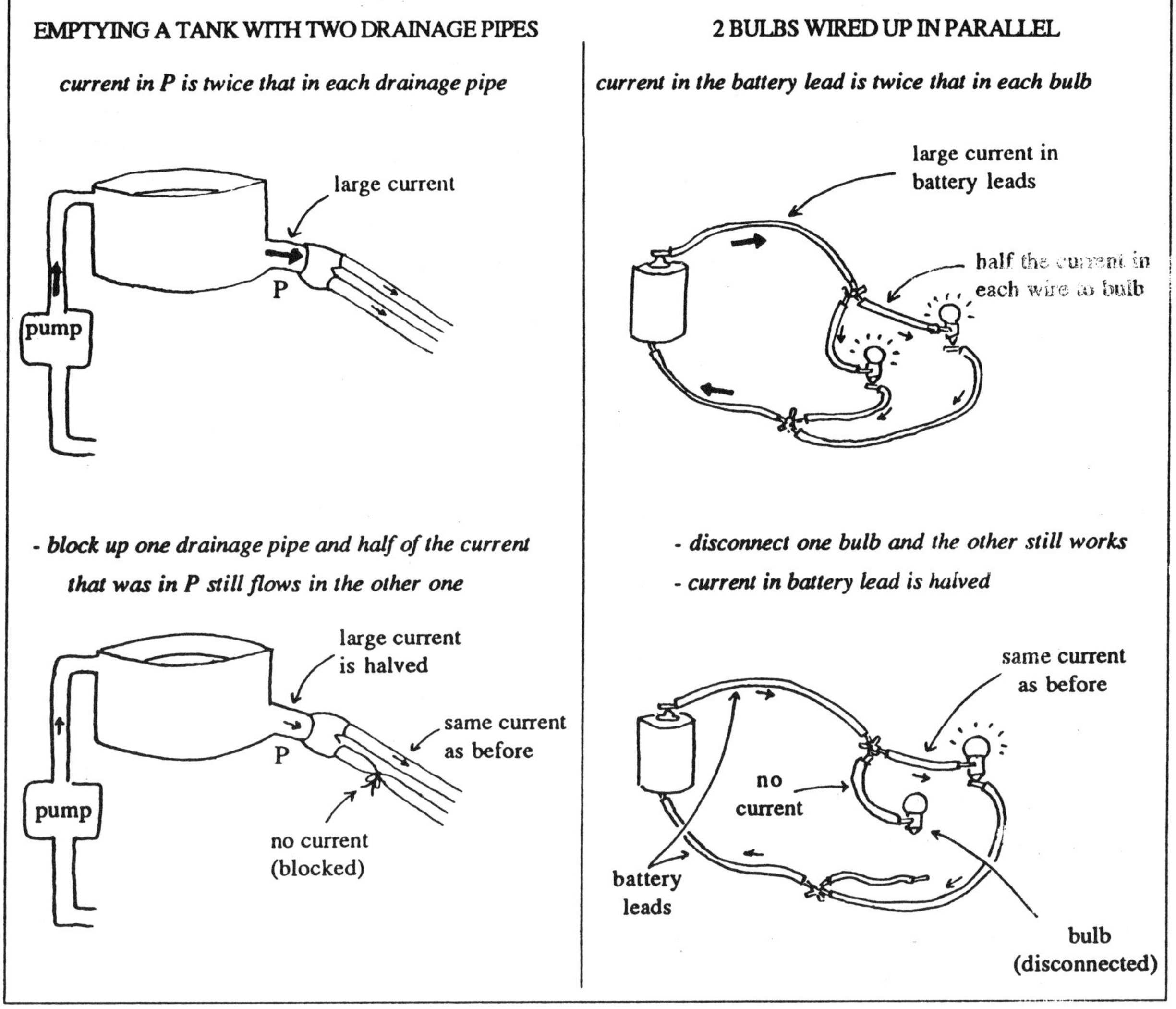

EMPTYING A TANK WITH TWO DRAINAGE PIPES

current in P is twice that in each drainage pipe

2 BULBS WIRED UP IN PARALLEL

current in the battery lead is twice that in each bulb

large current

large current in battery leads

half the current in each wire to bulb

pump

P

- *block up one drainage pipe and half of the current*

that was in P still flows in the other one

- *disconnect one bulb and the other still works*

- *current in battery lead is halved*

large current is halved

same current as before

same current as before

pump

P

no current (blocked)

no current

battery leads

bulb (disconnected)

Lucy's evaluation of children's learning of these objectives was optimistic. Analysis of 27 children's tests showed that post teaching:

- for Objective 2, in six test situations, all children did imply a flow-change due to resistors by mentioning different brightness or loudness. Only 4 children in the class explicitly described such a flow-change in their test (e.g. 'electricity is lessened' or 'controlled' etc).

- for Objective 3, in one test situation, 6 children implied that there was more power or electricity from the direction of the battery when wired in parallel, but only 3 described an increased flow of electrons or current in the battery lead.

- for Objective 4, in one test situation (Fig 27 below), 14 children wired up a 2-bulb parallel circuit successfully and seven also expressed the independence of the bulbs in some way. Three of the latter also had this understanding before being taught, so it was only four children's test scores which indicated effective teaching of this objective.

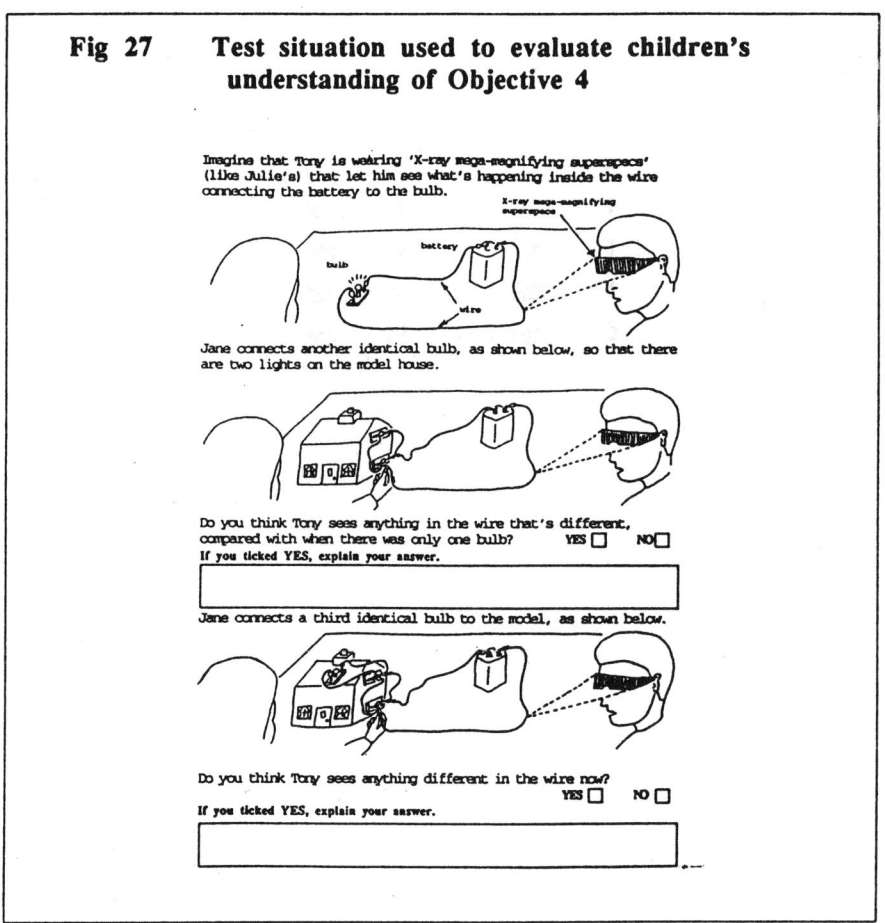

Fig 27   Test situation used to evaluate children's understanding of Objective 4

SUMMARY

Lucy's subject knowledge and the teaching knowledge she used in her sessions is summarised in Table 7 (next page).

FURTHER COMMENTARY

Lucy's teaching was not as effective as that of Joan's described in the previous chapter. Her own assessment of the effectiveness of her teaching was both over- and under-optimistic in terms of some conceptual gains she thought children had made. However, Lucy was also realistic in her recognition of mistakes made and of children's lack of progress in some areas. Although Lucy also had clear objectives and some personal confidence in the subject matter to be taught, aspects of her teaching contrasted strongly with features displayed by Joan.

Her intention expressed during planning to place more emphasis on 'input and knowledge' and less time on experimenting freely with the equipment was not realised - in fact the reverse happened. Children were given too much equipment on their desks at the start which tempted them to try out all manner of interconnections. This was really play rather than structured activity and it achieved little effect beyond familiarising the children with the equipment. This is of some value but the problem is that some of the interconnections made can damage certain components (e.g. blow a bulb or run down batteries very quickly). Had Lucy been aware of these technological pitfalls, which are an aspect of subject knowledge she had obviously not retained from her training, these exploratory activities could have been more controlled.

Items of equipment need to be introduced in a more gradual, structured way if they are to produce focused activity and successful outcomes (e.g. bulbs lighting, motors working). As in the case of Joan, this does show how technological problems can be an important issue for primary teachers. Lucy used two sets of equipment which were not compatible since one was designed to work with 1.5 volt batteries and the other with 6 volt batteries. These were mixed up and given to the children all together. Deeper subject knowledge might have helped to avoid this problem, but this could be an unrealistic expectation. More realistically, teachers can use components designed to work together (perhaps a commercial kit), and themselves try out experiments in advance to be aware of problems which may arise.

Table 7   Subject and teaching knowledge used by Lucy

SUBJECT KNOWLEDGE	TEACHING KNOWLEDGE
A circuit must form a complete pathway for an electrical device to work.	(1) Get children to build circuits and control them using switches. (2) Show drawing of a pathway (or 'circuit') on a handout - emphasise completeness. (3) Explain pathway in terms of electron flow. (4) Get children to predict whether different circuits (on a worksheet) will light a bulb.
A circuit can be series (in line) or parallel (branching).	(1) Get children to build a circuit with a motor and bulb in series. (2) Demonstrate to whole class how: a. 2 bulbs in series are dimmer than 1 alone. b. to assemble a parallel circuit (with 2 bulbs).
The branches of a parallel circuit are like separate independent circuits	Show how 2 bulbs in parallel are as bright as 1 alone (with same battery) - emphasise how the battery works separately on each bulb by means of stacking leads - children then do this.
An electric current consists of electrons already present in the circuit, moving in one direction.	(1) Marbles in the jar analogy. (2) Bicycle chain analogy: pedals are like 'the force of the battery'.
The size of the current is determined by the devices in the circuit and is measured with an ammeter.	(1) Get children to notice the effect on bulbs, buzzers etc when connected in the same circuit. Explain in terms of electron flow. (2) Get children to investigate size of current at different parts of the circuit with an ammeter.
In a parallel circuit the size of the current in the battery leads increases as more branches are added to the circuit.	Get children to investigate size of current at different parts of the circuit using an ammeter.
Circuits can be represented by circuit diagrams using symbols.	(1) Show component symbols (handout), get the children to match each item with its symbol. (2) Explain symbols *on equipment* - show how to put them into a circuit diagram. (3) Get children to match drawings of real-life circuits with their respective circuit diagrams. (4) Get children to interpret circuit diagrams and predict what will happen in them.

Lucy's teaching knowledge had the following features:

- use of analogy, but this needed more depth and mention made of its limitations. Also, this was done in a non-interactive way with children not being involved or engaged sufficiently. The marbles in the horizontal glass jar to illustrate the electrons already in the wire, and upturning the jar to indicate how all the electrons start moving together, was a useful aid. The limitation of this comparison is that the marbles all pile up at the bottom and leave the top of the jar empty, which was not described. The more comprehensive bicycle chain analogy which proved so effective in Joan's teaching was mentioned, but only verbally in passing and was given little emphasis.

- elicitation of children's views in an initial 'whole class' question and answer sequence. This seemed to be done for its own sake - Lucy did not use the responses as a starting point for developing the children's views by challenging and exploring them. Lucy did realise that she 'didn't ask them enough questions' which was because of pressure of time but also because she was 'a little bit concerned that I might not be able to answer them' due to 'my own lack of security in the subject'.

- the worksheets used were photocopied from published material. The content of these dealt with an idea which it seems most children already possessed, the circuit as a pathway, and with procedural knowledge. Children gained little understanding from them of the new concepts about current and electrons that Lucy was teaching.

- Lucy did have a range of activities planned which were relevant to her objectives, but the practical organisation and technological difficulties arising from the ways in which these were introduced and managed (see above) led to too much unproductive activity, and a lack of conceptual focus.

- use of appropriate language was a key issue for Lucy in her planning and her reflections showed her concerns about this aspect of her teaching. In this first attempt, the language she used often lacked the precision of the scientist as she struggled to convey these, for her, new ideas to the children. So, for example, 'In a parallel circuit you are letting each bulb have an equal amount of electrons' could suggest that bulbs use up electrons - a consumption idea. A form of words is needed that conveys the notion of a flow of electrons as current, and that it is the current which is the same in each bulb. Other examples are given in the text (see, for example, page 47).

- as described above, Lucy's goal was to place more emphasis on ideas rather than just procedures. While she did indeed introduce scientific concepts in short bursts of whole class teaching, there was too little emphasis on misconceptions that children are known to often have. Lucy had been introduced to the notion of electricity being 'used up' during the inservice programme but didn't 'think any of them had that idea'. Her worry about 'putting down' a particularly sensitive child by challenging his idea of bulbs 'sharing current' was understandable but skilful questioning can avoid this difficulty. The battery as 'a source of electricity' needed to be contrasted with the view of 'electricity as electrons' which she was teaching.

Post-lesson interviews with children suggested that these former ideas were still present and unchanged by the teaching. Similarly, when introducing the ammeter and how to use it in various circuits, there was insufficient emphasis on the way this should be done, which unfortunately resulted in confusion and the lack of comparability between the children's results described earlier.

- there was a lack of challenging questions aimed at the children and little discussion. Lucy's tendency to talk at the children could have resulted from the large size of the class but also perhaps reflected her worries about her ability to cope with questions from individuals.

AFTER TEACHING

Lucy's perceptions

The sections above entitled 'Lucy's comments' provide details of Lucy's views about her teaching. These were obtained from an interview after the teaching sequence was completed and also from her immediate reflections at the end of a session. Here, using these sources, we briefly summarise Lucy's views about:

(1) aspects of her teaching that went well.

She felt that children had been stimulated to go forward, had changed their ideas and made some gains both in understanding and in their use of language. She was rewarded by the pleasure children showed and had learnt some important lessons: groups chosen by ability were needed rather than whole class teaching; the objectives set were 'probably a bit too high' and there is a need to 'keep it simple' until you know the children's ability; any project set should be 'one they could actually cope with' - she felt that some children's ideas for models were technologically over-ambitious.

(2) whether her objectives were met.

Lucy thought that most children had grasped Objectives 1 to 4 but expressed reservations about their understanding with regard to some components (e.g. buzzers). She felt her teaching of the use of an ammeter (Objective 5) had been unsuccessful and was pessimistic about children's understanding of circuit diagrams (Objective 6) which she thought they found 'very hard'.

(3) particular difficulties she experienced.

Lucy was doubtful about the success of her teaching but admitted that this was a subjective feeling not based on any objective assessment of children's learning. She mentioned her continuing insecurity in her subject knowledge which had led her to avoid general class questioning and discussion if possible. She had difficulty coping with some children's questions, or with understanding their ideas and felt this had led her into areas beyond her own subject knowledge and understanding. In spite of this she was prepared to 'have a go' by keeping one step ahead of the children and making an effort to learn about anything she 'doesn't know'.

Lucy recognised difficulties children had when using ammeters and had been puzzled by the unfamiliar phenomena which resulted from children's wrong connections. She also recognised that too many components had been made available at one time and felt that the children did not have as much 'basic knowledge' as she had assumed. She did not know what the children's misconceptions were but thought that no child had a 'consumption model' for current (Fig 7b). She had assumed that they knew about the completeness of the pathway and the effect of breaking it, but found that some were confused about the action of a switch.

(4) other issues.

Lucy generally varied her teaching style depending on the lesson. She felt that in the sessions observed children were using 'theory' she had provided followed by application of this to practical situations, but also were inductively deriving ideas from their practical experiences. However, Lucy did feel that at times children were trying to provide correct answers for her rather than striving to understand. She had tried to get the children to focus and be more structured and logical in their approach. She felt that management difficulties arising from the large number of children had affected her teaching of procedures and of concepts.

Lucy expressed a number of negative views and commented about the erosion of teachers' confidence in general in recent years and the negative mindset that adverse publicity about the teaching profession had produced.

SUMMARY

Lucy' teaching was not as effective as that of Joan (see the previous chapter). Children were not challenged to the same extent, and Lucy was less systematic in her introduction and reinforcement of both the use of equipment and ideas. A degree of success was achieved with some objectives, but less so than in Joan's case. Lucy's teaching knowledge was not as well developed as Joan's with insufficient emphasis on key points and known areas of difficulty, less precision and sometimes a little confusion in her use of language, elicitation which seemed to be for its own sake rather than as something to address and build on, and a less thorough exploration and explication of the analogies used.

It must of course be remembered that Lucy was dealing with a class of more than thirty children (not her own class) rather than, as in the case of Joan, a group of six. This inevitably restricted Lucy's ability to interact with individuals and made considerably greater demands on her. Even so, many differences in her approach did not seem to be linked in any obvious way to class size. In fact Lucy's class control and ability to maintain attention when necessary were outstanding. She had not taught electricity in this way before i.e. using an approach which has conceptual objectives and the introduction of ideas underpinning the behaviour of circuits. Her courage and willingness to attempt such a new approach under the eye of researchers and a colleague can only be admired. After the sessions she reflected with considerable insight on the approach she had taken and learnt much from the experience which will cetainly inform her future teaching.

CHAPTER 5

SARAH: A SCIENCE GRADUATE IN A PRIMARY SCHOOL

PROLOGUE: summary of scientific knowledge used in this case study

Circuit

A circuit must form a complete pathway for an electrical device to work. It can be a series (in line) or parallel (branching) circuit and can be opened or closed by switches. Parallel is better because bulbs are brighter when in parallel than when in series and one bulb can be removed without affecting the other(s). Circuits can be represented by circuit diagrams using symbols.

Electric current and electrons

An electric current consists of electrons, already present in the circuit, moving in one direction. Its size is indicated by the brightness of a bulb or loudness of a buzzer and can be measured by an ammeter.

Battery and volts

The battery provides the push for the electrons to move. The size of the push is measured in volts and determines the brightness of a bulb in a circuit.

Conductors and insulators

The atoms of conductors have 'free' electrons which can form an electric current. Atoms of insulators do not have free electrons.

ABOUT SARAH

Sarah was a chemistry graduate who had been trained to teach juniors during her PGCE course in the 1970s. After a few years teaching in a variety of schools, including children with special needs in a secondary school, she obtained her present post in a Junior and Infant school of 225 children, many with special needs. The school's catchment area is mixed and includes a social priority area. She taught infants for the first 4 years and had spent the last 12 years teaching upper juniors. For 5 years she had acted as the school's science coordinator when her concern had been 'other things than subject knowledge - more (to do with) activities and experiments'. Sarah became the school's deputy head 6 years ago and now held responsibility for coordinating mathematics teaching in the school. She was a full-time class teacher of 33 children, 21 of whom were Year 6 and the rest year 5, teaching all subjects in the curriculum.

In her own schooling in North America she had studied biology, physics and chemistry to grade 13 which she described as 'somewhere between GCSE and A-level'. She had attended various Local Education Authority training courses prior to the introduction of the National Curriculum (1988) and described the aim of these as 'doing science that is more than just nature study'.

BEFORE TEACHING

Sarah's objectives and the children's learning

Table 7 shows Sarah's fourteen objectives i.e. the ideas she wanted her Year 6 children to acquire. Each child's understanding of an idea before and after teaching was investigated by means of a written test, with an in-depth interview also for 6 of them, and expressed on a scale from 0 (little or no understanding), through 1 (some understanding) to 2 (good understanding).

Changes in mean scores of the sixteen Year 6 children taught, for all objectives (Table 7), show that Sarah's teaching varied in effectiveness. Children gained some ideas about electrons (Objectives 3, 4, 5, 6 and 9) which were completely absent before teaching and this was quite marked in the children interviewed (see Appendix IV). Before teaching, some objectives (10 and 14) seemed to be better understood than others (1, 2, 8 and 11) - post-teaching scores for

Table 7 Changes in understanding of Sarah's 16 Year 6 children

TEACHER'S OBJECTIVES Children should understand that:	CHILDREN'S MEAN SCORE	
	Pre-teaching	Post-teaching
1. a complete circuit, including a cell, is needed for an electrical device to work.	0.88	1.19
2. battery-holders and bulb-holders are a convenient way of completing the pathway which constitutes the circuit.	0.38	1.06
3. an electric current consists of electrons, already present in the circuit, moving in one direction.	0	0.56
4. the battery provides the push for the electrons to move.	0	0.81
5. the amount of push from a battery can vary.	0	0.88
6. the size of the push from a battery is measured in volts.	0	0.81
7. an electric current's size is indicated by the brightness of a bulb or volume of a buzzer.	0	0.33
8. the amount of electric current is measured by an ammeter.	0.44	0.88
9. substances with 'free' electrons are conductors but those without are insulators.	0	0.75
10. a switch opens or closes a circuit to allow a device to operate.	1.06	1.25
11. components in a circuit can be shown on paper as symbols (i.e. circuit diagrams).	0.81	1.5
12. the working of some devices (e.g. buzzers) depends on current direction.	0	0.25
13. a circuit connected in parallel is better than one in series because the bulbs are brighter and one bulb can be removed without affecting the other.	0	0.56
14. the voltage of a battery also determines the brightness of a bulb in a circuit.	1.63	2

KEY: 0 = little or no understanding   2 = good understanding (max. score)

all of these showed gains in understanding. The ideas Sarah taught least effectively were Objectives 7, 12 and 13.

Sarah's planning

Sarah's final aim was for her children to apply the understanding they achieved from her sessions to 'some little situations' she had invented to do with 'Toad of Toad Hall', a story the class had recently read and enjoyed very much. So, for example, one group were asked to wire up some extra lights for Mr Toad's car; another group were to devise a circuit to tell Badger that someone had come into his house, and so on (see Fig 28).

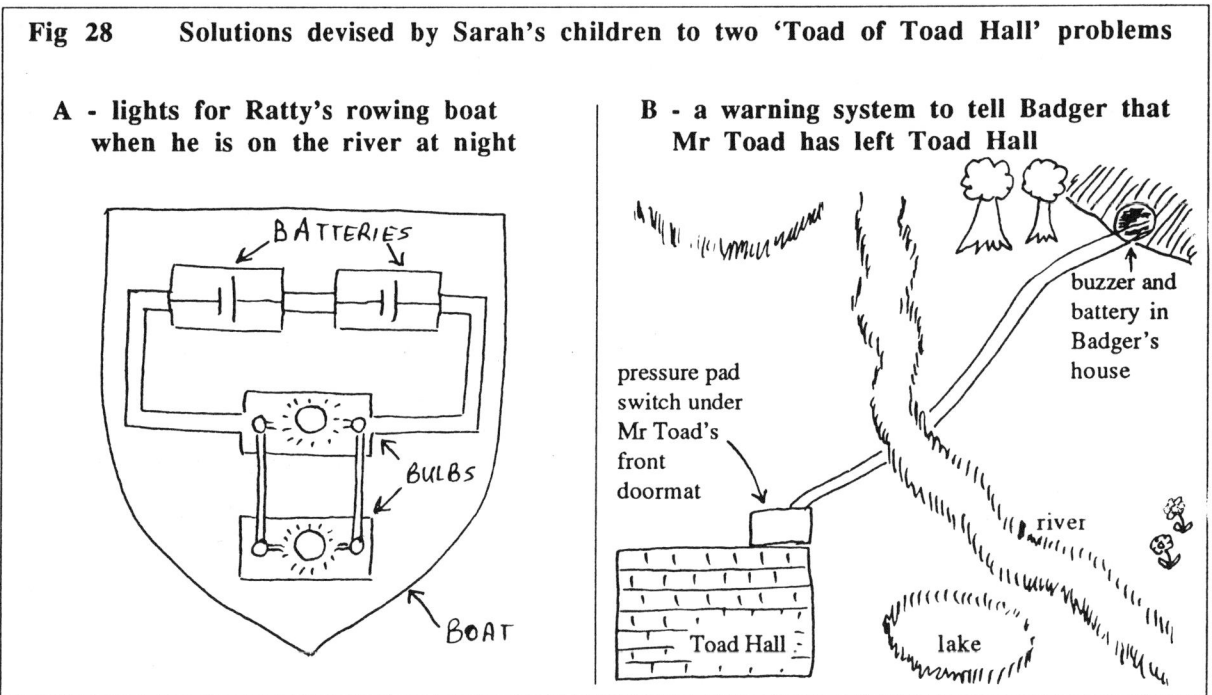

Fig 28   Solutions devised by Sarah's children to two 'Toad of Toad Hall' problems

A - lights for Ratty's rowing boat when he is on the river at night

BATTERIES

BULBS

BOAT

B - a warning system to tell Badger that Mr Toad has left Toad Hall

buzzer and battery in Badger's house

pressure pad switch under Mr Toad's front doormat

Toad Hall

river

lake

To achieve this aim, Sarah's planning strategy was to:

- 'first think of the order that things had to come'.
- next think of the practical aspects - 'what would be the best way of working with children to get the points across?'.
- devise a 'sort of general introduction' - necessary since this topic was new to the children.
- explain issues to do with safety.
- 'remind them of things they may have done or that they already know'.
- provide 'easy straightforward hands-on activities' at work stations by means of two circuses (in sessions 2 and 3) around which the children would circulate.
- follow each circus with a whole class discussion addressing not only *what* happened in each work-station activity but *why*. Sarah stressed her wish to go beyond mere observation and, by providing explanations, try to develop children's understanding.
- introduce the 'Toad Hall' projects to the children in which they could apply knowledge they

had gained from circus activities to solve problems.

• have a final feedback session in which children could inspect each other's solutions to the 'Toad Hall' projects, just as Sarah herself had done with her colleagues' projects during the training received at the start of the research.

In devising the content of her sessions Sarah's principal source was the training pack ('Current Understanding') used during her INSET. She took two approaches to choosing her objectives. Some were chosen as ideas worth learning for their own sake, for which suitable activities would have to be devised:

Teacher: .. some objectives I was thinking yes, at the end of the day I would like them to sit down and be learning this .. Some things were obvious objectives and I thought, 'What experiments or activities would I like to be giving the children a chance to do to help them understand this?'

Other objectives were chosen as ideas children needed for a practical project she had planned:

Teacher: I was also thinking of some practical activities (*i.e. Toad of Toad Hall projects*) that I would like them to be doing and also try to match up what knowledge I need to be imparting to back those activities up.

She felt the level at which she had set her objectives was within the capabilities of her children but that not many of them would have much prior understanding of the ideas to be taught:

Teacher: I think they're not going to understand very much (*i.e. before the teaching starts*). I'd be quite surprised if they do understand anything. I can't see that they would have learned that at school.

When discussing objectives with the research team, she wondered 'whether I am taking on too much' in her desire to teach the children about current in series and parallel circuits. She used her judgment to limit this objective (number 13) merely to understanding that one arrangement (in parallel) is 'better' than the other (in series) - see Table 7. However, analogies concerned with current in series and parallel circuits which she had met during her training (e.g. Fig 46, Appendix V) had, she felt, given her more confidence in her own subject knowledge and she was keen to try them out with the children. When she asked the researchers for guidance about this, it was pointed out that she was entering 'unknown territory':

Interviewer: It would be very interesting if you taught that and found that children simply could not cope. It would not be a reflection on your teaching but a very interesting research finding. If you taught it and found that some children did cope, that is also very interesting. I don't want to dissuade you from doing things that you feel maybe they could cope with. This is where your judgment comes in. If you feel happy about teaching it that's fine. Whatever you feel you want to do we will find very interesting because (perhaps) no one has done this before with children of this age.

71

In fact Sarah did try to teach ideas about the size of current in a series and parallel circuits but there was no evidence that this was effective (see later).

She felt 'a lot more confident than I ever was (before)' especially in her theoretical understanding of those ideas covered during training which she intended to teach. She thought her understanding of these had been consolidated or improved and much of this was due to the analogies used which gave her more confidence to try to explain or 'to help children to see it'.

Sarah still had some reservations about her understanding of certain ideas, and about the practical side of the teaching. However, her confidence to 'have a go' was boosted by the 'nice equipment' provided which she felt eliminated doubts (always there when using the 'scissors and sellotape' approach) that a circuit might not be working because of bad connections:

Teacher: I have been grateful (that the training has let me) .. think again about practical equipment in a different way .. this plug-in equipment .. seems to eliminate the problem of equipment getting in the way of some learning going on. I was taken by that so much .. it's been a real eye-opener.

It did become noticeable how quickly both Sarah and the children developed a facility with, and a faith in, the equipment so that much time was spent on discussing and considering the workings of circuits rather than on worrying about faulty connections.

Sarah's approach was to provide practical activities to get children 'intrigued and interested' and for this she designed her own worksheets with some material taken directly from the INSET package 'Current Understanding'. She also used a little published material as extension work for early finishers. She would follow this practical activity with whole-class teaching and discussion but did not think children could induce or discover the notion of electrons. Since electrons were to be used as an important explanatory tool, they would have to be taught first:

Teacher: (The idea of electrons) is something that people have to sort of accept. I haven't got any idea of electrons except that I know they exist .. in varying amounts, those 'free' electrons (*Objective 9*). I think that should be the level which the children are at. That has to be a taught thing.
Interviewer: They are not likely to discover that from activities.
Teacher: No, I think one would be trying to use that as an explanation for some of these phenomena .. (from) that set of experiments (in each circus) .. discussing what happened with all those ..

Sarah thought her approach to teaching electricity was now 'completely different' because 'this isn't a subject I've taught well before' and she had 'never really attempted to explain anything (before) - it's been purely on observation.'

A constraint on her planning was the limited time available but she explained that, in response to the researchers' exhortation to be ambitious, she had deliberately planned a 'challenging' sequence of sessions 'to see what happens, for me and for you' (i.e. the researchers).

How the children responded to this challenge will be seen in the sections which follow.

THE TEACHING

Overview of teaching sequence
While her 12 Year 5 children were being supervised elsewhere by a colleague, Sarah taught a sequence of five sessions over a period of seven days to 21 Year 6 children (9 boys and 12 girls). Only 16 of these were present for both the pre- and post-teaching written tests. The six children chosen by Sarah to be interviewed by the researchers were described by her as 'all not far away from average' with 'no real high fliers'.

The main focus and content of each session are summarised below.

• *Session 1 (45 mins)*
  - safety; language;
  links between words;
  plugs and sockets
  (introduction).
	A story was told about an accident with mains electricity and its dangers were stressed. The safety of school equipment was explained - also procedures for connecting up the equipment. A 'brainstorming' session elicited some of the children's existing knowledge about electricity.

• *Session 2 (1 hr 45 mins)*
  - circus of 5 activities;
  a whole class discussion
  of relevant ideas
  (objectives 1, 2, 3, 4, 5,
  6, 9, 11 and 12).
	Activity 1: understanding the pathway in bulb- and cell-holders.
	Activity 2: ways to stop a bulb lighting ('gaps' in the pathway).
	Activity 3: putting conductors/insulators in gaps in the pathway.
	Activity 4: reversing connections to components - do they work?
	Activity 5: make a real-life circuit from a diagram and vice-versa.
	Ideas: pathway, diagram conventions, atoms, electrons ('free' in conductors), current direction, the battery pushes electrons.

• *Session 3 (1 hr 45 mins)*
  - circus of 4 activities;
  a whole class discussion
  of relevant ideas
  (objectives 7, 8, 10,
  13 and 14).
	Activity 1: using an ammeter to measure current in the circuit.
	Activity 2: effect of adding an extra bulb in a series circuit.
	Activity 3: effect of adding an extra bulb to a parallel circuit.
	Activity 4: testing different types of switch in a circuit.
	'Rest' station: for reflection on the words/activities met so far.
	Ideas: size of current in a simple circuit (using an ammeter), why connecting bulbs 'in parallel' is better than 'in series', a switch is an open/closed 'gap'.

• *Session 4 (one hour)*
  - Session 3 ideas (contd)
  starting a practical project.
	Current in series and parallel circuits, electrons and resistance. In groups - designing a circuit to solve a 'Toad of Toad Hall' problem, considering the equipment needed to build it.

73

• *Session 5 (one hour)*	Building the solutions to the 'Toad Hall' problems (Toad's
-feedback; sharing project	car etc), presentation and discussion of solutions and of what
solutions; recap of content.	has been learned, quiz to test understanding, safety again.

How did Sarah achieve her objectives?

An analysis of the results of Sarah's efforts to achieve her 14 objectives (Table 7) with the sixteen children taught shows four main findings:

1. the teaching of ideas about *electrons* showed some effectiveness.
2. teaching the circuit as a *pathway* which can have *'gaps'* in it was also partly effective.
3. teaching ideas about the *direction* of electric current was less effective.
4. ideas involving the *size* of the current in circuits were rather less effectively taught.

What follows is an account of some subject knowledge and teaching knowledge Sarah showed in her teaching of these ideas which has not been described for Joan or Lucy.

1. IDEAS ABOUT ELECTRONS

Four of Sarah's objectives (3, 4, 5 and 9) involved the notion of electrons - a completely new idea to her children. In Session 2, during a whole class discussion of the battery's role in a circuit, the bicycle chain analogy was introduced using an upturned bicycle loaned by another member of staff. Without using any visual aid other than the bicycle, she introduced the concept of electrons:

Teacher: This is a thought that you can't see so you need to focus: all materials are made of atoms; in the middle of each atom is a centre called a nucleus; there is something around the edge called electrons.

The greater freedom of these electrons to move in some materials compared with others (see Table 7, Objective 9) was described and applied to develop the children's understanding of their earlier experience of conductors and insulators in the circus activity:

Teacher: In some materials, like plastic, the electrons are held on tight. In copper, like in the wire, they are held loosely. So in the things that allowed the electricity to pass (*Circus Activity 3*) the electrons are held loosely.

Sarah now introduced the idea that the *entire circuit* contained these electrons:

Teacher: In a circuit all the way round, in all the wire, the metal parts in the holders and bulb and battery,

74

all these are full of electrons. Just like the bike chain has got links all the way around, these metal parts (*of the circuit*) have got electrons all the way round sitting there waiting to work.

To emphasise the simultaneous movement of electrons at all points around the circuit when it is connected, Sarah asked three children to focus on what happens to links at different places on the chain at the instant she begins to move the pedals (Fig 29):

Children: They all start moving at the same time.

Fig 29   Teaching knowledge used by Sarah to show how electrons at all points in the circuit start to move simultaneously when the circuit is connected

The battery's role as an 'instantaneous' pusher of electrons which were already there in the circuit was then taught in terms of the bicycle chain analogy:

Teacher: What are they (*the electrons*) waiting for? The battery. When we put the battery in it starts all the electrons moving. Thinking back to the bike, what provides the push that made the 3 children's links (*see Fig 29*) move at the same time?

Children: The pedals.

Teacher: So the chain is to show you a kind of mockup of what it might be like inside the circuit where we can't see .. batteries can be bigger or smaller, can have more push to them. What's the word (for) the amount of push a battery's got?

Children: Volts.

This notion of voltage as an indication of the amount of push of the battery was logically quite consistent with the children's existing belief (either intuitively held or obtained from previous experience), shown by the scores for Objective 14 in Table 7, that the battery's voltage determines the brightness of a bulb in the circuit.

During the discussion and practical sessions which followed, Sarah constantly re-visited these 'two really hard ideas, that electrons are in everything and that some things hold on to electrons better than others', using them and the other ideas about electrons which she had introduced as an explanatory tool.

2. THE CIRCUIT AS A PATHWAY WHICH CAN HAVE 'GAPS' IN IT

The children had some prior understanding of Objective 1 - the need for a complete circuit, including a battery, for an electrical device to work (Table 7). Sarah developed this in several ways.

Firstly, she ensured that children were aware of the extension of this idea to the bulb- and battery-holders in the new equipment they were using. At one of the circus work stations children were specifically asked to trace the continuation of the electrical pathway between wires and the bulb or the battery through the inner parts of the holders (Fig 30):

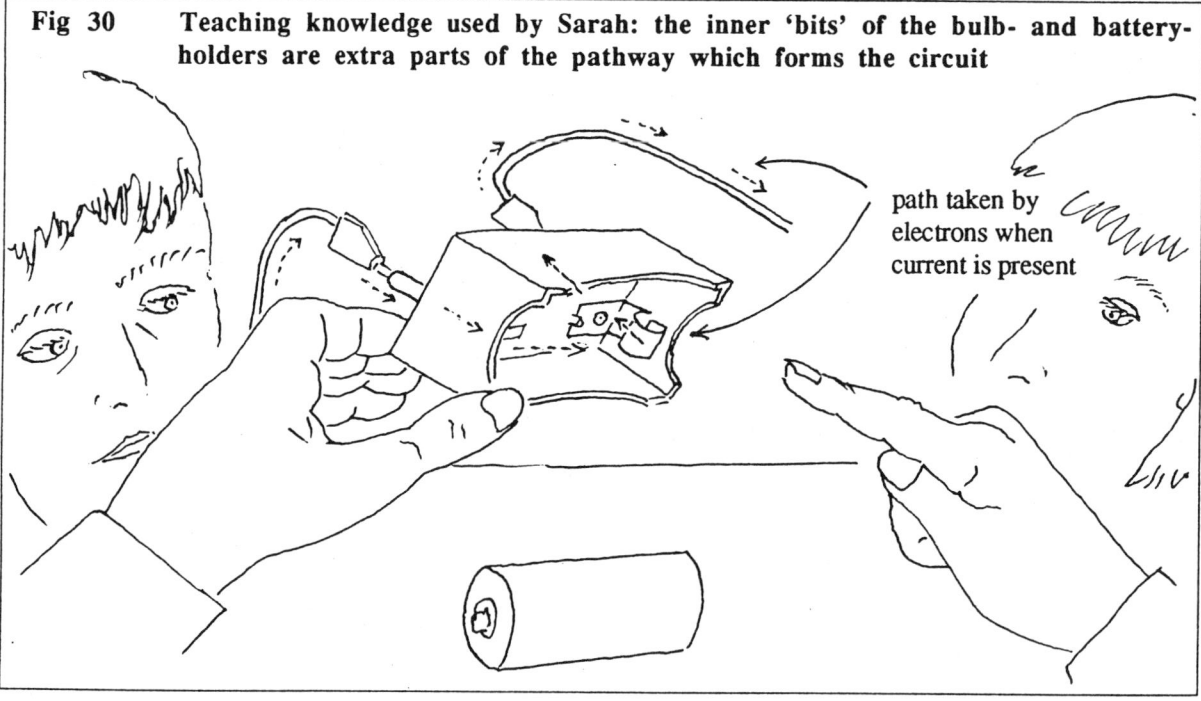

Fig 30   **Teaching knowledge used by Sarah: the inner 'bits' of the bulb- and battery-holders are extra parts of the pathway which forms the circuit**

path taken by electrons when current is present

Teacher: Look inside the holder. When you join up you plug (the wire's plug) into here (*i.e. the battery holder's connecting socket*). Where does that (socket) go inside? Can you see the metal springy bit? .. when we use the battery holder it's as if these (*i.e. the sockets*) were the top and bottom of the battery - it's all joined up with metal. Can you see it's the same with the bulb holder? You have told me the bulb only lights if one wire touches the bottom and the other touches the side (of the bulb). I want you to convince yourself that this thing, the bulb holder, does that. When you put the bulb into the bulb-holder, it's like when the wires (themselves) touch the bulb.

76

Secondly, Sarah re-interpreted the pathway idea in terms of conductors and electrons - for example, when going through a list of children's ideas about electricity which she had obtained from an initial brainstorming session:

Teacher:	First word - 'Circuit'. what's important about it? What can we say that's more than a word?
Jack:	A circuit is sort of like a full thing round with no breaks in it.
Teacher:	You can use the word full pathway. Pathway of what?
Jack:	A conductor.
Teacher:	.. what about wires?
Jack:	They are conductors.
Teacher:	What do we know about conductors and their electrons? Do they hold on to them tightly or are they the kind that can get pushed around?

A further development of this idea of a pathway was to include the notion of a 'gap' in the circuit which stopped it working because it was not complete. A circus activity was provided in which children tried to find as many ways as possible of creating a gap in the pathway of a simple circuit containing a bulb, a battery and two wires. During discussion of this activity, Sarah illustrated the possibilities on the board by successively erasing different parts of the circuit (Fig 31).

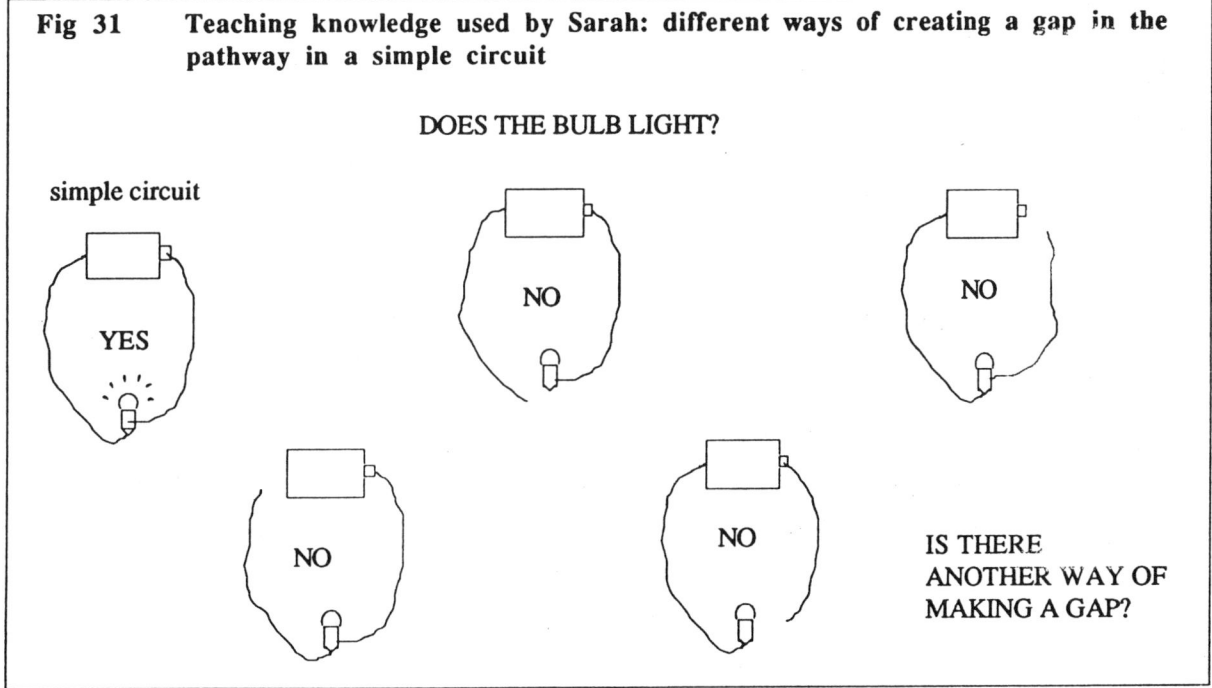

Fig 31   Teaching knowledge used by Sarah: different ways of creating a gap in the pathway in a simple circuit

DOES THE BULB LIGHT?

simple circuit

YES

NO

NO

NO

NO

IS THERE ANOTHER WAY OF MAKING A GAP?

Sarah also used appropriate language when teaching this idea, refering to the bits of the bulb and battery which it 'is important to touch on to' (i.e. the terminals) in order to make the pathway complete.

At another work station, Sarah gave children an activity for investigating conductors and insulators in which it was emphasised that it is a gap in the circuit which is being filled by each substance tested. One child's response showed the importance of not making assumptions about children's understanding of this apparently simple concept:

Zena: What's the gap?
Teacher: The gap is this, Zena. At the moment air is in it.

In this way the children were led to the idea that a conductor was something which, when it filled a gap in the circuit, allowed the bulb to light - a 'complete pathway' perspective in addition to the 'free electrons' model which Sarah had introduced.

The concept of a switch as a gap in the pathway which is filled with air (an insulator) when open (i.e. 'off') or filled with the metal part of the switch (a conductor) when closed (i.e. 'on') was a further development of the pathway idea which Sarah used effectively. In the second circus (Session 3) children were given a variety of switches to use in a simple circuit. In the reed switch, the gap closes visibly and audibly when a magnet is brought near (Fig 32).

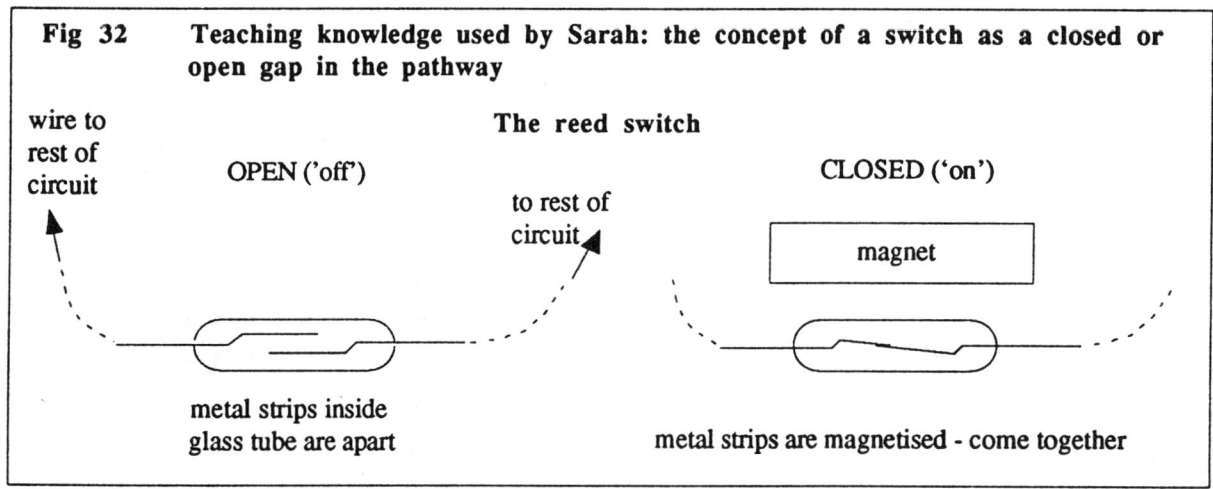

Fig 32   Teaching knowledge used by Sarah: the concept of a switch as a closed or open gap in the pathway

Teacher: This is a funny kind of switch called a reed switch. Look carefully inside that glass tube and you can see 2 bits of metal only a tiny way apart. If you use this magnet you can hear a tiny click if you're close. That click is the 2 bits of metal just touching each other. When that happens it means there is a pathway there through it .. see inside how the 2 bits of metal are separate and you've got to use the magnet to bring them together.

The gap within a push switch (Fig 33) is hidden inside the structure but Sarah taught it in terms of a conductor closing a gap inside when pushed. She also used the 'hat' circuit diagram symbol which the children had seen painted on the base of the switch, drawing it on the board to illustrate what must be happening inside the switch when it is pushed:

78

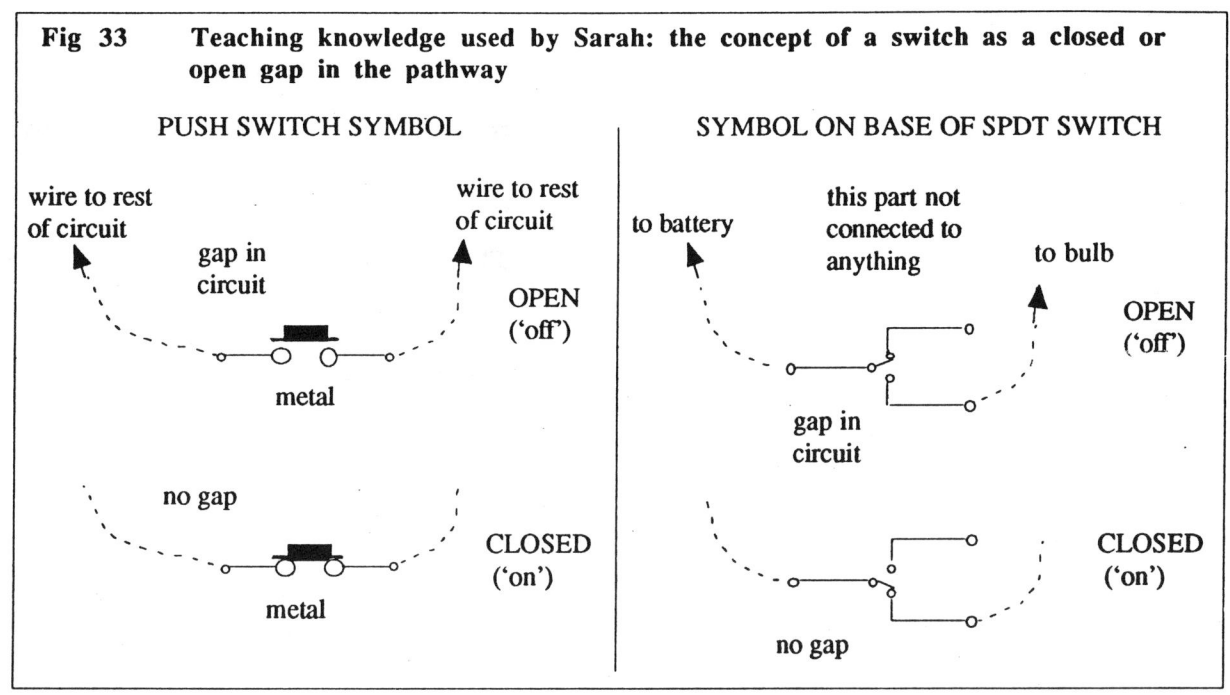

Fig 33 Teaching knowledge used by Sarah: the concept of a switch as a closed or open gap in the pathway

PUSH SWITCH SYMBOL	SYMBOL ON BASE OF SPDT SWITCH

Teacher: Right now I'm not touching it and the light's not working. Why is that?

Steven: Because you're not pushing.

Teacher: But what happens inside when we do push?

Steven: The electricity starts to work.

Teacher: Yes, because we have completed the pathway, so what must be there now?

Steven: Electrons, power.

Teacher: Remember the experiment last week when we had conductors and insulators going in the gap? .. *(removes the switch and holds the 2 wires apart)* Did air allow the electricity to pass through?

Steven: No it's the wires.

Teacher: The switch is a bit like that *(re-connects it)*. Inside there must be a little bit of metal. At the moment *(switch not pushed)* there must be a gap like this, only (it is) inside the switch. Now *(pushes the switch)* we are closing the gap.

Steven: Then the gap closes and turns the bulb on.

Similarly, the gap within a 'click switch' was pointed out to the children in the circuit diagram symbol painted on the base of the 'single pole double throw' (SPDT) switch (Fig 33):

Teacher: Can you see on here - the little diagram? It's meant to show you what it's like inside. When it's pressed down in this position *(CLOSED)* this side is allowing the pathway to be complete. We've brought that flap over to here so we've made a pathway from the battery through here to the bulb.

(she turns switch to OPEN position)

> When it's going here, it's going nowhere - we've broken the pathway, made a gap .. when we closed (the switch) we made the light work.

Both of these symbols were new to the children but they possessed the idea of circuit symbols as representations of real-life objects before the teaching began (Table 7 Objective 11), and so could accept the use of a symbol to convey some aspect of the object it represented.

Sarah taught the different uses of the push switch and 'click switch' (SPDT switch) with a vivid illustration: she asked children to imagine having to stay by the classroom door all day with their finger on a push switch if the school used these to operate the lights. This seemed to be an effective approach since most of the children interviewed contrasted the temporary nature of the push switch with the permanent effect of the SPDT switch.

Something much enjoyed by the children was a pressure pad switch. Sarah described the squeezing of the pad in terms of a gap inside it being closed and this seemed to be an effective and useful addition to the range of other switches she had introduced. Fig 24B shows how one group of children incorporated a pressure pad switch into their Toad of Toad Hall project.

The work with switches definitely captured the children's imaginations, as shown by the range of ideas they proposed during discussion for applying switches to real-life situations. For example:

Dean: It (*the pressure pad*) could be by my friend's front door so his light comes on when he goes in.
Zaquar: You could put it (*a push switch*) on the door and when he tries to push it, the alarm goes off.

Objectives which Sarah taught less effectively

3. CURRENT DIRECTION

Sarah's objective was for the children to understand merely that current has *a direction* rather than the particular direction defined by the scientist:

Interviewer: How are you going to describe the direction to them - in what terms?
Teacher: I don't think I had in mind thinking about the battery, a positive and negative end, but more that certain devices will work, you know, only one way round in the circuit.

She gave the children a 'more challenging' activity in which they investigated the directional nature of devices. Children first investigated whether a bulb worked when its connections to the battery (now out of the holder to clarify how it was connected) were reversed (Fig 34).

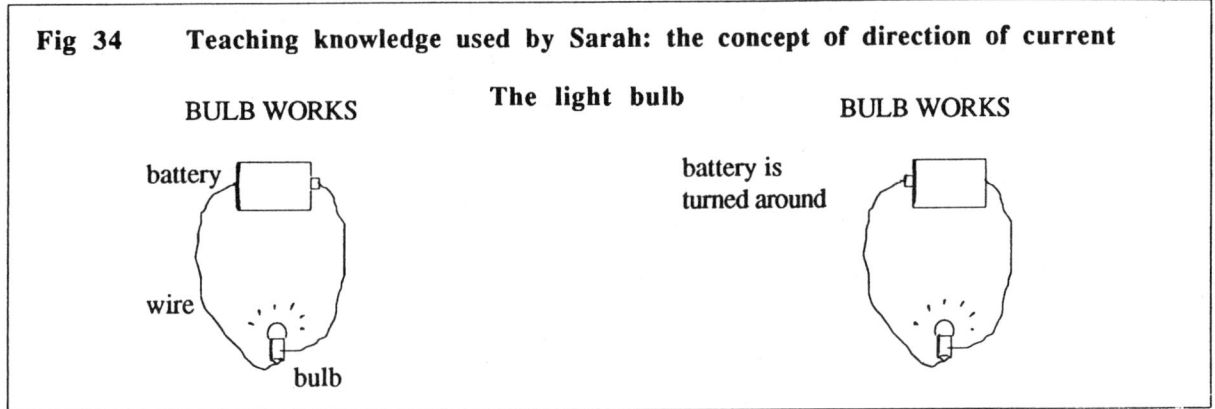

Fig 34 Teaching knowledge used by Sarah: the concept of direction of current

The light bulb

BULB WORKS — battery, wire, bulb

BULB WORKS — battery is turned around

With a motor, children obtained a different result (Fig 35):

Teacher: What happened with the motor when you changed round the connections to the battery?

Heather: It still worked.

Teacher: The same way?

Heather: No, the little thing (*motor's shaft at the side*) went (*i.e. revolved*) the other way round.

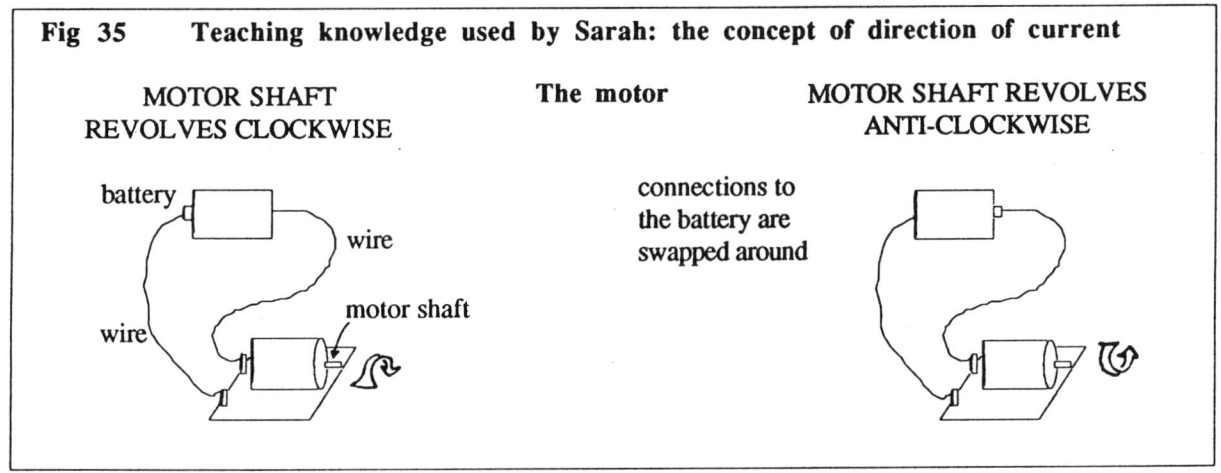

Fig 35 Teaching knowledge used by Sarah: the concept of direction of current

The motor

MOTOR SHAFT REVOLVES CLOCKWISE — battery, wire, motor shaft

MOTOR SHAFT REVOLVES ANTI-CLOCKWISE — connections to the battery are swapped around

In the case of the buzzer, children saw that if it worked when connected in a certain way, it would cease to work when the connections to it were swapped over, and vice-versa (Fig 36).

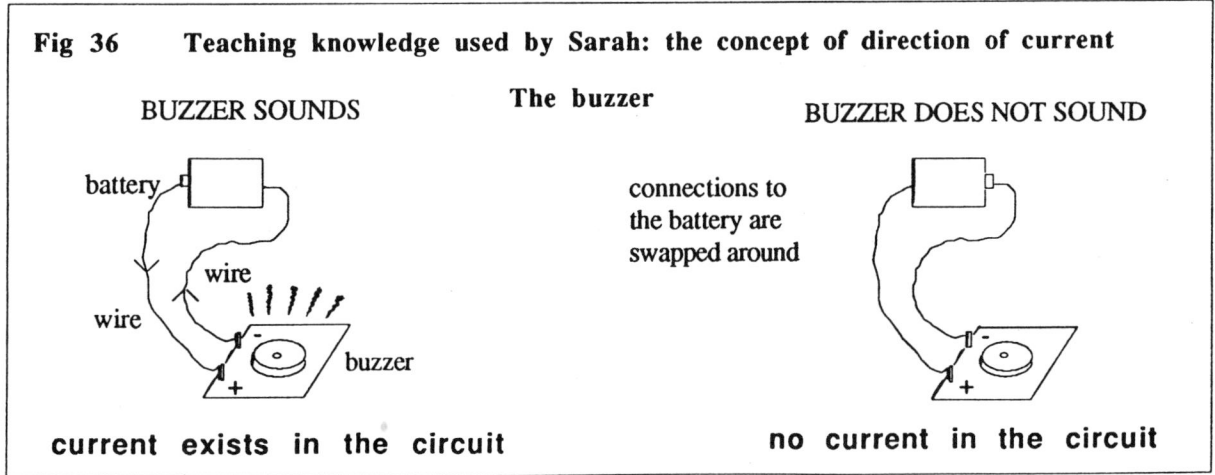

Fig 36 Teaching knowledge used by Sarah: the concept of direction of current

The buzzer

BUZZER SOUNDS — battery, wire, buzzer

BUZZER DOES NOT SOUND — connections to the battery are swapped around

current exists in the circuit

no current in the circuit

This can be explained as the buzzer being so constructed that it only conducts in one direction (in fact when the electron current is from the buzzer's minus terminal to the plus terminal). Sarah supplied an explanation to the children during the discussion session after the circus:

Teacher: What about the buzzer?

Ricky: It stopped when you changed it round.

Teacher: So the buzzer stopped when you change it round. What does that tell us? - that the electric current goes in a direction and for some of the devices it matters which way round the current is going. Some of them don't mind, like the bulb, but some do mind and they will only work if the current is going one way through it.

Sarah's explanation implies that current can be in either direction in the buzzer but that it only sounds for one of these directions - which is a misconception. In fact the buzzer only conducts in one direction i.e. when the battery is the right way round. Hence the buzzer can be used to identify the current direction in a circuit. This lack of clarity may help to explain Sarah's limited success with this objective. Sarah repeated the directional aspect of current by teaching that a battery pushes electrons. She reinforced this by continually emphasising the need for all the pushes of the batteries to be in the same direction when connected together in series, which was a common source of puzzlement to children whose equipment would not work (Fig 37):

Teacher: (*sees the children's circuit is not working*)Well now have you built your - ? Um, for a start you need to line the batteries up. See how .. in the little sketch (*i.e. circuit diagram provided*) it goes short-long-short-long? We've got to match it up the same in real life, so that's the problem.

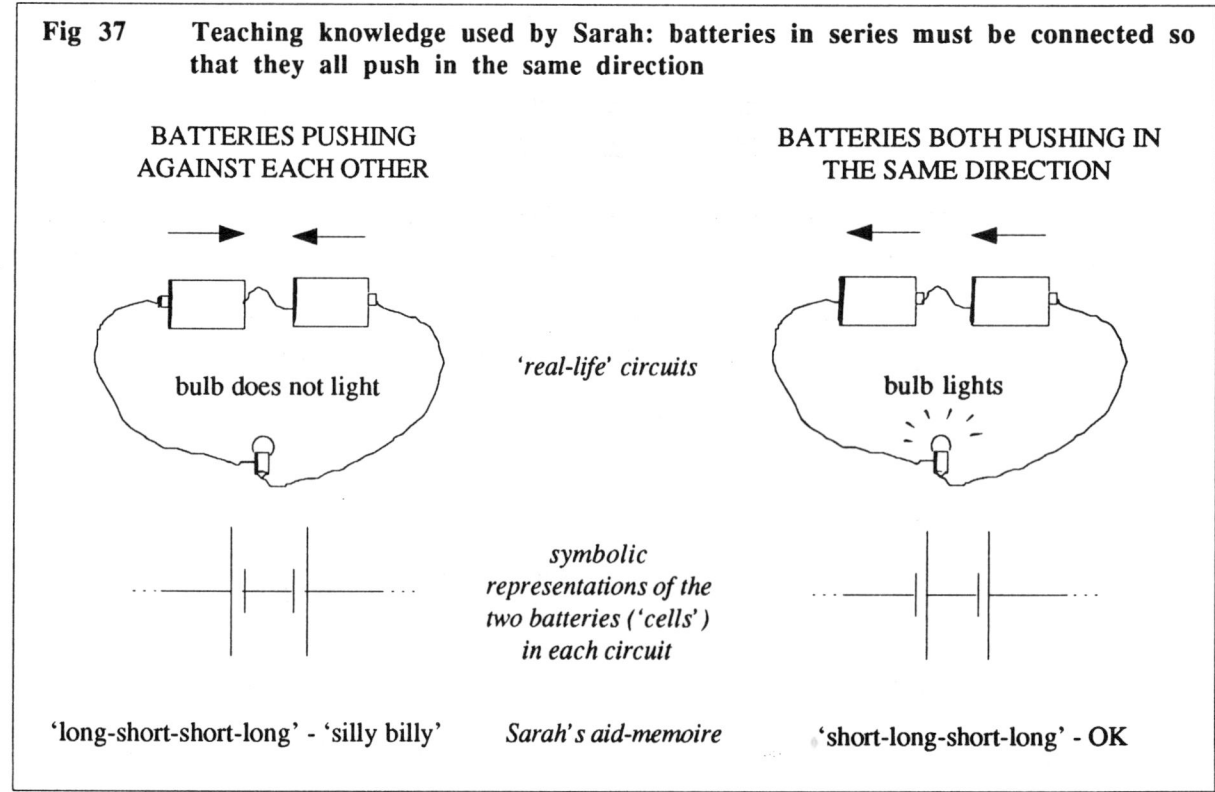

Fig 37   Teaching knowledge used by Sarah: batteries in series must be connected so that they all push in the same direction

BATTERIES PUSHING AGAINST EACH OTHER

BATTERIES BOTH PUSHING IN THE SAME DIRECTION

bulb does not light

'real-life' circuits

bulb lights

symbolic representations of the two batteries ('cells') in each circuit

'long-short-short-long' - 'silly billy'

Sarah's aid-memoire

'short-long-short-long' - OK

Sarah herself committed this error on one occasion but soon diagnosed the problem:

Sandra: We can't do it.

Teacher: OK where is your other battery? It says use 2 batteries (*connects them in series*) Now you press .. (*it doesn't work*) Let's just check. What's happening here? Hold on, make sure the metal's touching - let's try again (*it doesn't work*) Let's try another wire (*it doesn't work*) So what's the matter here? Ah! Can you see what's the matter? I've just spotted it. Something with the batteries. (I'm a) silly billy! The batteries have got to line up. Look - see the way they're marked with that long and short line? They've always got to be the same way round or they're cancelling each other out and working against each other - (I'm a) silly billy!

Sarah conveyed this subject knowledge with some teaching knowledge of her own:

Teacher: If I give my push this way and (Lorna) gave her push towards me, would we be going anywhere?

Children: No!

Teacher: .. if you want your two batteries to work together you've got to have them lined up together, rather like if Lorna lined up beside me and we both pushed the same way, we're giving more push. If we pushed against each other, we're basically cancelling each other out.

4. THE SIZE OF THE CURRENT IN CIRCUITS

Sarah's teaching of this aspect of electric current seemed the least effective (see scores for Objectives 7 and 8 in Table 7). The teaching knowledge she used is briefly described here.

At a circus work station children used a current-measuring meter ('ammeter') to investigate the size of the current in each wire, A and B, of a simple circuit (see Fig 38).

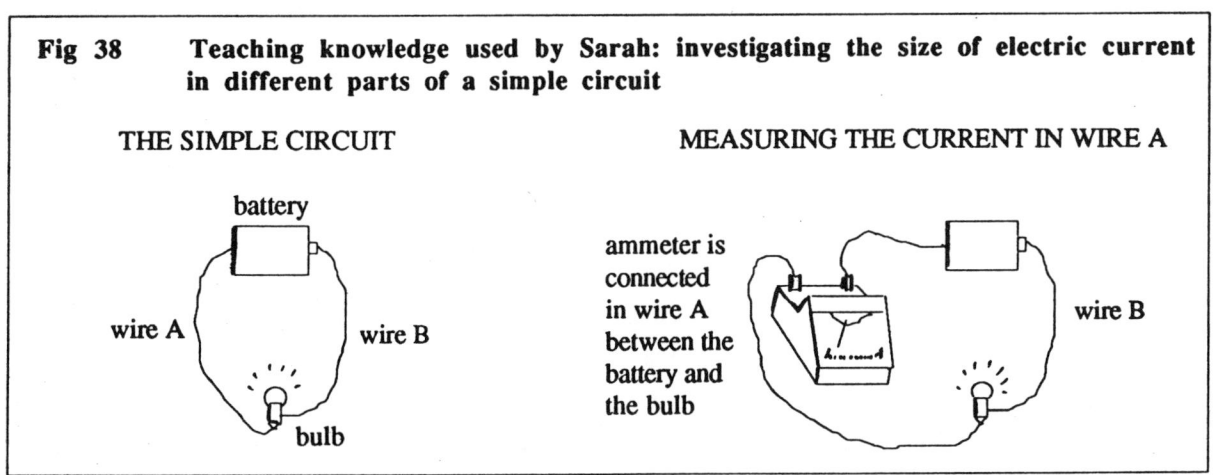

Fig 38   Teaching knowledge used by Sarah: investigating the size of electric current in different parts of a simple circuit

Children were told about the ammeter's function and shown how to insert it into the circuit:

Teacher: It's called an ammeter and it measures how much electric current is flowing through the circuit .. electric current makes the needle move .. We can't cut the wire (to put in the ammeter) so we plug it in (and add another wire). It matters which way round it's plugged in so if it isn't working at all, switch the leads around please. The way it's useful is we can see if the electric current is the same all the way around the circuit.

Children were asked to note the reading of the ammeter in each position. Rather than asking them to interpret the equal readings for themselves the worksheet provided the conclusion.

Teacher: First record what happens - work through in a logical sensible order. What's the next thing? (*gets the child to connect the ammeter into the other side of the circuit*) It (*i.e. the ammeter reading*) is the same! The worksheet says, (*reads*) 'If the ammeter reading is the same at A and B' - at both sides if you like - (*continues reading*) 'that shows the flow of electrons and the electric current is the same all round the circuit. Is this true?'

Sarah then suggested adding to the circuit an extra battery 'that's going to give more push' and asked children to predict if (a) the ammeter reading would be the same as before and (b) it would be the same on both sides of the circuit.

In the above sequence, Sarah's subject and teaching knowledge are both sound. Why, then, did the children learn little about the size of electric current in circuits? We shall consider this issue in the Commentary section of this chapter.

Summary
Sarah's teaching of objectives concerned with ideas about electrons and the circuit as a pathway with switches acting as gaps in it was partly effective, as was that concerned with ideas about the direction of electric current (though slightly less so). Objectives to do with the size of the electric current were least effectively taught. Teaching knowledge used in her more effective teaching is shown in Table 8 (next page).

COMMENTARY

Planning
Sarah's planning was extremely thorough and enabled her to deliver a coherent teaching sequence in which the important issue of safety was dealt with at the outset and some elicitation of children's prior scientific knowledge was to take place (see later). Her two group activity sessions were highly structured and showed a progression from easier to more difficult topics. In the whole class sessions following these, ideas relevant to the activities were presented and discussed. A cross-curricular theme, Toad of Toad Hall, enabled children to use their newly learned skills and ideas in designing and constructing a practical application.

When planning, Sarah debated with herself whether to teach children about the size of the current in series and parallel circuits. She had doubts about this and adopted a simpler objective which was merely that parallel circuits are 'better'. However, in Session 4, she did attempt to teach the more difficult ideas and so went beyond her original plan. A possible effect of this is discussed below.

Table 8   Subject knowledge and effective teaching knowledge used by Sarah

SUBJECT KNOWLEDGE	TEACHING KNOWLEDGE
Battery- and bulb-holders are a convenient way of completing the pathway which constitutes the circuit.	Ask children to trace the continuation of the electrical pathway between wires and bulb or battery through the inner parts of the holders.
An electric current consists of electrons which are all pushed simultaneously by the battery when the circuit is switched on.	Bicycle chain analogy: get several children each to focus on a particular link (= electron) at the moment the pedal (= battery) is pushed.
The size of the push depends on the voltage of the battery.	Discussion of how the size of battery voltage is related to their push.
Electric current is the same all around a simple circuit.	Investigate size of current in each lead using a current-measuring meter (ammeter).
In some materials (insulators) electrons are not free to move - in others (conductors) they are 'free'.	Relate this idea to each substance which makes the bulb light (or doesn't do so) when placed across a gap in a simple circuit.
The entire circuit contains electrons (including insulators).	Bicycle chain analogy: emphasise how the *whole* bicycle chain is made up of links.
A complete circuit is needed for an electrical device to work.	Ask children to demonstrate different ways of making a gap in a simple circuit and emphasise the effect of doing this.
A switch is a gap in the pathway filled with air (an insulator) when open ('off') and by a metal (a conductor) when closed ('on').	1. Let children experience a reed switch. 2. Explain the gap in a push switch and SPDT switch using the circuit diagram symbols.
Electric current has a direction.	1. Get children to investigate directional nature of a bulb, motor and buzzer. 2. Resultant effect of pushes by 2 cells in series.

Subject knowledge

The sessions showed that the confidence Sarah expressed in her subject knowledge for those areas she chose to teach was, on the whole, well founded. The only evidence of uncertainty or lack of understanding on her part about the particular aspects of electricity she wished the children to understand was in her explanation of current direction within the buzzer.

Teaching knowledge

To achieve her objectives Sarah used a range of strategies whose effectiveness (see Table 7) is discussed here.

• The bicycle chain analogy was used by Sarah in two sessions and she regularly referred to it. Four of the six children interviewed cited this analogy as a reason for their learning about various aspects of the circuit involving electrons, and reference to electrons was made by two non-interviewees when asked to compare a circuit to a bicycle chain in an example from the pencil and paper test. Others wrote in their test papers that a bicycle chain resembled a circuit because 'it made things go'. Thus the analogy seemed to be effective for different children at different levels.

- The circus is a useful pedagogic strategy which can provide a succession of interesting and stimulating experiences prior to discussion and explanation of them. However, it does result in a loss of the immediacy that comes from talking about events as they occur. This delay between activity and explanation could lessen the impact and does make demands on children's recall.

A further drawback of the circus approach is seen when work-station activities are conceptually sequential. In the first circus, the concepts of (a) a complete pathway, (b) making 'gaps' in the pathway, and (c) filling these gaps with substances were presented. The desired logical order (a-b-c) was only available to children starting at Activities 1, 4 and 5, with the others, starting on Activities 2 and 3, meeting the ideas out of sequence as they moved around the work-stations. Such considerations may have decreased the effectiveness of Sarah's teaching in the case of some objectives.

- Although Sarah herself knew that an electric current consists of moving electrons, she sometimes used a form of words that did not make this clear. For example:

Teacher: .. with the plastic .. they (the electrons) won't move so easily - they do not allow the current to pass through it.

More frequent emphasis that the moving electrons *are* the electric current might have made her teaching of this point more effective.

- Sarah elicitated children's prior knowledge in the introductory session by getting them to 'brainstorm' words to do with electricity and then asking them to suggest any ways in which the words were linked. This is a 'concept-mapping' technique which can give useful insights into the way children are thinking.

Sarah probed more deeply into children's prior ideas about switches but did not do this systematically for all her objectives or explore in detail children's views about what is happening within a circuit. However she did aim specifically to refute the 'consumption of current' misconception (Fig 7b, Chapter 3) with an ammeter by means of Circus Activity 1. Also the bicycle chain analogy does refute any idea of 'clashing currents' within the circuit. In spite of this, after teaching, one of the six children interviewed thought that electrons were 'used up' by the bulb. This demonstrates the obstinacy of these previously held intuitive ideas and shows perhaps that an activity plus deduction is not enough for some individuals - they also need to engage in debate about their views before changing them.

- As with the teachers in the previous case studies, Sarah met some problems arising from technological properties of the equipment such as having the correct battery voltage for particular components. On one occasion she solved this by applying her subject knowledge: when a buzzer was placed in series with two bulbs, it sounded but the bulbs failed to light. She deduced that this must be because the battery is 'not giving enough push' (in fact, a current was present - sufficient to operate the buzzer - but it was not large enough to make the bulb filaments glow). Sarah knew that a larger current would be present in a parallel arrangement and so tried that, which succeeded in making all three components work.

- Sarah's plan for Objective 13 was merely for the children to understand that parallel circuits 'are better' for wiring up lights than series ones. This is because bulbs in parallel remain at the same brightness as more are added (if added in series they become dimmer) and also stay on if one is removed (in series all bulbs stop working when one is removed).

In Session 4 she went beyond this original planning and tried to explain *why* this happens in terms of the size of the current in the circuits. Since the research investigated only those objectives the teachers had planned, the effectiveness of this teaching cannot be directly assessed. However it is likely from the children's low scores for the simplified objective (see Table 7 - Objective 13) that it was ineffective. Why might this be? Perhaps it is because this subject knowledge is beyond the capabilities of children of this age. Alternatively, it might be that these ideas *can* be understood by 11 year olds but that Sarah's children did not manage this due to some other factor.

Some of the teaching knowledge Sarah used for this (see Appendix V) was taken from the training she had received, which had been effective in improving her subject knowledge. She also used 'water-in-a-pipe' analogies of her own. Sarah expounded these analogies to the children quite rapidly in about 25 minutes, moving from one analogy to another in her explanation. This is probably far too brief a time for children to assimilate the ideas involved and it might have been wiser to use a single analogy at a time. It may be that they became confused and this affected their ability to comprehend the far simpler idea - merely that parallel circuits were 'better' - that Sarah had originally planned to teach.

- This rapid teaching and mixing of analogies may have had another effect. Sarah's main strategy for teaching children about the role of the ammeter (Objective 8, Table 7) was an apparently straightforward Circus Activity (number 1) in Session 3. Their understanding of this might also have been affected by the confusion described above.

Further points

- The relationship between current size and bulb brightness (Objective 7) seems fairly straightforward and Sarah's ineffectiveness in teaching this was puzzling. It may be that it was a new idea, involving a fresh concept - 'current', which was, as it were, competing with the children's (correct) prior intuitive knowledge that bulb brightness depends on battery voltage (see scores for Objective 14 - Table 7). She did suggest that children measure the current when a higher voltage battery was connected (which they predicted would increase the brightness of the bulb). However, no emphasis was placed on the larger *current* that is present to distinguish this idea from what might seem to a child a rather similar notion involving voltage.

- The notion of 'free' electrons (Objective 9) was taught by relating the idea to tests the children made of substances which conduct or insulate. Sarah verbally stressed the idea of 'holding on to electrons loosely or tightly' and most children understood that this had something to do with electrical conductivity. However some were not clear about which type of substance (i.e. conductors or insulators) had the free electrons.

  Perhaps an additional activity or visual demonstration is needed to clarify this and produce fuller understanding.

- When Sarah asked the whole class about the direction of electric current (objective 12) during discussion only a single child responded. The children did not seem to fully understand the link between a device not working and the electric current having a direction. Again, perhaps a further activity or analogy is needed to clarify this (Fig 39).

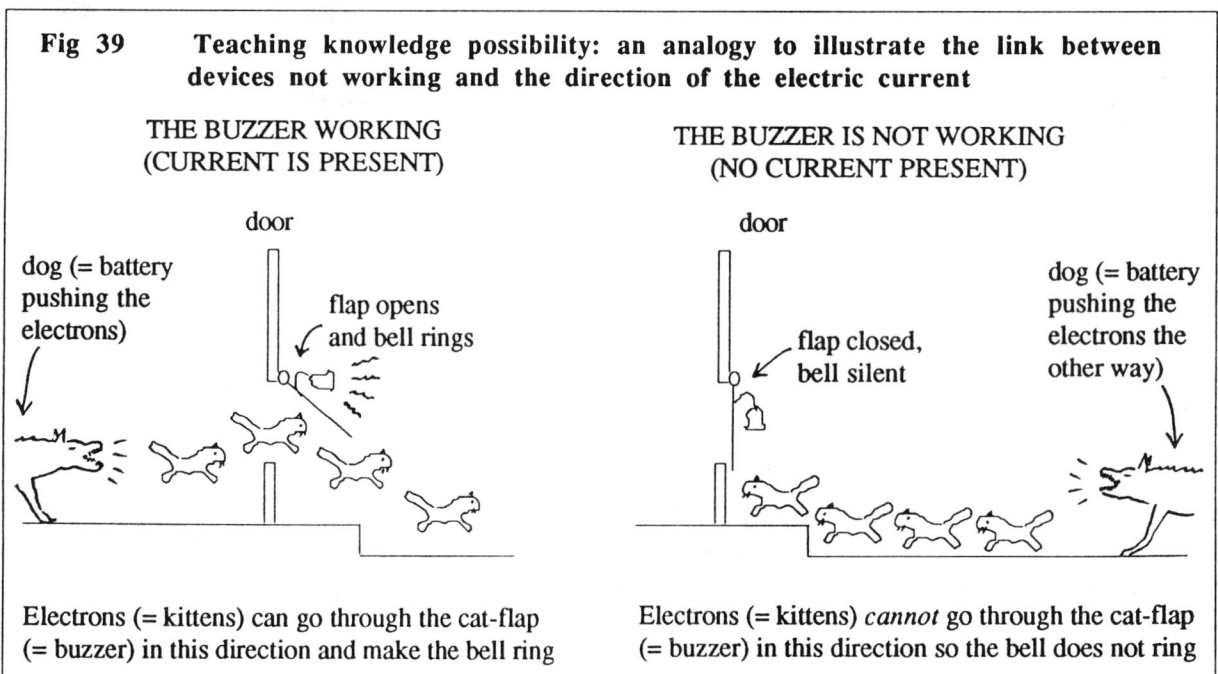

Fig 39   Teaching knowledge possibility: an analogy to illustrate the link between devices not working and the direction of the electric current

THE BUZZER WORKING
(CURRENT IS PRESENT)

door

dog (= battery pushing the electrons)

flap opens and bell rings

Electrons (= kittens) can go through the cat-flap (= buzzer) in this direction and make the bell ring

THE BUZZER IS NOT WORKING
(NO CURRENT PRESENT)

door

flap closed, bell silent

dog (= battery pushing the electrons the other way)

Electrons (= kittens) *cannot* go through the cat-flap (= buzzer) in this direction so the bell does not ring

Some other characteristics of Sarah's teaching

- She used frequent repetition and emphasis of the ideas introduced in a range of contexts.

- She was able to simplify ideas by using language appropriate to the children's experience.

- She showed good practice in clearing away non-essential equipment and arranging circuit components to convey the ideas represented in the circuit diagram.

- Sarah showed empathy with children in the language she used in her explanations e.g.

> Teacher: (a parallel circuit is like) .. adding another layer, piggy-back almost, on to the first circuit. (With a series circuit).. think of it as a circle and you keep adding more and more things into the circle.

However she did use scientific language ('grown up' words) such as 'parallel circuit' because she felt that 'means something because the children have experienced it'.

- Sarah's discussion sessions were sometimes rather 'one-way' with the emphasis on children giving the required answer rather than on exploring their own ideas. This may have been because of time pressure. In a normal classroom situation she would be able to proceed at a rate more in keeping with the children's grasp of the ideas she was teaching. She was certainly sufficiently experienced and sensitive to the children's needs to be aware of where they were, but pressed on, perhaps to keep to the research schedule. On one particularly hot afternoon, she kept the children going when normally she would probably have eased off and changed to a less demanding activity.

AFTER TEACHING

Sarah's perceptions

After completing the teaching sequence, Sarah talked to the research team about:

(1) aspects of her teaching which she thought had worked well.

Sarah felt that she had been successful in terms of her overall plan of

> Teacher: .. some practical activities followed by discussion and building on to a second set of practical activities and then trying, although it was a bit rushed, to put it into practice (*with the Toad of Toad Hall activities*) .. the whole thing seemed to make some sense.

Her increasing familiarity with the equipment had enabled her to become more at ease and less stressed as the sessions progressed - she referred (jocularly) to 'dying a thousand deaths' and 'a bit of a nightmare' early in the teaching sequence! Her teaching of the bicycle chain analogy had, she thought, been effective and 'vital' because it 'seemed so simple' and let her 'make simple connections between things'.

The final Toad of Toad Hall practical work enabled her to see if the children really did have the understanding she hoped they would get from the circus activities. The problem-solving aspect of this project work led children into 'a technology area' which was worthwhile since it built on the ideas taught in the circuses and made them seem practically relevant.

(2) children's understanding of the objectives she had set.

Sarah was not sure about the effectiveness of her teaching of the complete circuit idea (Objective 1) because of her inability to tease from the children the word 'complete' to describe the pathway. She was 'a bit disappointed' about this because she thought the children's understanding of this 'would have been really firm in their minds'. However, this might have been a language problem for the children in addition to any conceptual difficulties they were experiencing.

Other areas she felt doubtful about were Objective 8 (the ammeter as a device to measure electric current) and Objective 9 (free electrons as an explanation for conductors and insulators). Although Sarah felt that the bicycle chain was 'certainly a powerful analogy for children' she was not sure 'whether they got the complete idea of the analogy' in respect of the notion that electric current is the same all round a simple circuit.

She was also dubious about her teaching of current in parallel circuits (an extension of Objective 13) using the water pipes analogy (see Fig 46, Appendix V) and of resistance in the light bulbs. The latter was not a planned objective but she did attempt to teach it in terms of electrons having to 'squeeze through the bulb's narrow filament'. She also thought that the effect on the pathway of unscrewing a bulb was not always clear for some children.

Although children's grasp of a lot of ideas was 'a bit delicate' and it 'wouldn't be too hard to trick them', Sarah felt that she had effectively taught circuit symbols (Objective 11), using switches (Objective 10), the battery as a pusher of electrons (Objective 4) and, with reservations about some children, electric current in terms of electrons (Objective 3). From the Table 7 scores her judgment would seem to be a little on the optimistic side.

Sarah felt that the children 'had cottoned on' to the practical aspects of parallel circuits, i.e. using parallel circuits in project work, but was unsure 'whether they can show you that from diagrams'. She was pleased with their procedural knowledge of how to construct a complete circuit, how to use the equipment in general and also how to manipulate equipment to diagnose circuit faults. Sarah felt that the children found the equipment satisfying because

Teacher: .. it eliminated the uncertainties (about bad connections) so you can begin to see more clearly where the problems are. That for me as a learner I found so useful and I'm sure it was true for the children .. I think you have to be quite certain that the circuit you are trying to build is working.

In the future she said she would get children to use the equipment as a design tool to construct the correct circuit for a practical project and then they could translate that into wires and components that fit on to the actual model that they were making.

(3) difficulties she had encountered.

Sarah had some management problems with individual pupils and also a few difficulties using the equipment (which did not seem to affect her enthusiasm for it); she admitted that on one occasion when she introduced a 6 volt battery into a circuit 'it was fingers crossed that I didn't blow everything'. She also admitted to uncertainty about some ideas that had been taught during the INSET (e.g. 'what is going on in the battery') and to ephemeral understanding of others which she did not specify:

Teacher: .. there are some ideas where .. I would know something one minute and be uncertain the next.

However she felt that she had few difficulties in terms of her subject knowledge during the sessions because she had selected ideas that she 'felt most confident with' to teach to the children.

(4) the level of the objectives she taught in relation to the children's age and ability.

Sarah thought that the children had enjoyed the lessons because they 'felt special' and their efforts had been valued by her and the researchers. She felt that both her objectives and the equipment she had selected were appropriate and interesting for 11 year olds who were

Teacher: .. quite capable of all that I was doing in these sessions .. I left out some things that I didn't, for one reason or another, want to do and most of it was really to do with the children. If you had long enough, they could learn more, be pushed on more.

However, she also admitted that her assessment of the children's learning might not correspond to reality and looked forward to some feedback about this from the research:

Teacher: .. as a teacher you can be very pleased with how certain things went and realise that other things were perhaps a bit more uncertain and .. you can be so sure that they must have got this idea, that it all went well, and we all know it might not have - so it will be interesting (to find out how the children's understanding changed).

(5) whether children's misconceptions had been addressed.

When asked about this, Sarah seemed to misunderstand the question and referred to the final quiz in Session 5 where

Teacher: .. there was a couple of occasions where someone had got the wrong idea or had missed the point and that was an occasion to try and put the right point to them, like Richard who forgot the bit where all materials were being made up of electrons - he had forgotten so it was a point to directly put right.

Sarah emphasisied that during the sessions she had constantly tried to explain to the children *why* things went wrong in their circuits rather than 'just fixing it and leaving it'.

(6) how typical of her teaching in general this approach was.

In maths and language, Sarah would normally teach groups, with an activity for each and the children moving from one to another on a weekly basis. Previously, she would not have taught electricity in the way observed in this research but might in the future set up 'something rather similar' with perhaps half the class (or smaller groups if the amount of equipment was a constraint) going round a circus of activities while the rest did something else. After swapping there would then be 'a teaching session all together'.

Sarah felt that putting the children under pressure by giving them only 10 minutes at each work station and demanding a group presentation of project work after an elapsed period worked well. She would definitely not have the whole class doing group activities at the same time since she felt that children 'need the teacher, not with them but nearby' when they got into difficulties. If she were unable to 'spread herself around effectively' she worried that the activites, which were directed ones with an expected outcome, would 'degenerate into playing with the equipment'.

Sarah said that she had enjoyed being part of the research project which, she felt,

Teacher: .. has taken me forward a long way and is going to make me here in the classroom a better teacher next time we do this topic, there is no question.

She attributed this to her increased confidence in her subject knowledge which had enabled her to 'try and extend some of the ideas to the children'. She felt that while teaching she was occasionally 'not much ahead of the children and puzzling things out with them'; also that she was often at the limit of her subject knowledge but that this knowledge had been consolidated.

Sarah was very positive about the approach taken by the INSET pack:

Teacher: The fact that you have gone into the research side - what are people's misconceptions and so on - and that you have gone so carefully through all the activities which as a learner has made it very easy for me to learn a lot quickly .. must have something to do with the success of this book.

However, she did not feel that her pedagogy had been much affected by her training - the main influence of the training had been on her subject knowledge.

SUMMARY

Sarah's confidence to teach electricity had greatly increased as a result of the training she had received. She was keen to teach with an emphasis on explanation and understanding. This was a new approach for her. She planned, thoroughly and meticulously, an ambitious series of lessons with a demanding list of objectives.

Her teaching of objectives concerned with electrons showed some effectiveness, as did that which developed the idea of a circuit as a complete pathway with switches creating a gap which can be closed in the pathway. The objectives concerned with current direction and size, and with parallel circuits, were less effectively taught. A possible reason for this was that in discussion and explanation too much was presented too quickly.

Sarah used and developed subject and teaching knowledge she had gained during her INSET training. She made extensive use of analogies, with some success, in particular the bicycle chain analogy for an electric circuit. The teaching sessions involved a series of highly structured group activities arranged in a circus followed by whole class discussions in which scientific ideas were presented to the class. Sarah was enthusiastic about the equipment used. Both she and the class quickly gained proficiency with it enabling the children to focus on what was happening in the circuits.

After the sessions Sarah looked back thoughtfully on her teaching. She felt she had learned enormously from the experience and that she would be able to build on what she had learned in the future.

CHAPTER 6

THE CHILDREN'S LEARNING

INTRODUCTION

This chapter examines the nature of the children's learning in more detail. Some of the major aspects of the learning are compared for all three case studies. This is followed by a more in depth description for one of the studies (the case of Joan). The chapter provides accounts of:

- the ideas and understanding the children had prior to teaching.
- how these developed into scientific understanding.
- the new scientific ideas which the children learnt successfully.
- suggestions for how the teaching could possibly have been developed to further enhance the learning.
- the factors to which the children attributed their learning.

HOW THE INFORMATION WAS GATHERED

The children whose learning was followed in more detail, and which is the subject of this chapter, were interviewed in depth before and after teaching. Each interview lasted about 30 minutes, and followed up, clarified and extended each child's responses to the pencil and paper test. The transcripts of the interviews for each child were analysed as follows. Firstly, the pre-teaching interview was read thoroughly and the characteristics of the child's understanding identified under the three headings:

- preconceptions - either a misconception, that is, a scientifically incorrect idea, or, a partially understood scientific idea.
- missing - a scientific idea for which there was no evidence of any knowledge or understanding.
- knows - a scientific idea of which the child demonstrated knowledge and understanding.

The post-teaching transcript was then read thoroughly. It was examined for evidence of the ideas and understanding the child now held. These were listed and classified as:

- scientific ideas
    - successfully acquired
    - partially acquired
    - incorrectly acquired
    - not acquired.
- unchanged ideas.

94

- chances for development.

'Chances for development' were where the children had developed their scientific understanding to some extent but where, in the view of the researchers, if the input from the teacher had been greater, or slightly different, there were opportunities to enhance that understanding.

The pre- and post-teaching ideas were listed next to each other to show what had become of each of the pre-teaching ideas and how the child's understanding had developed. Summary sheets for each child were produced (see Appendix III for an example). In addition the reasons given by the children for their learning were noted.

WHAT THE CHILDREN LEARNT SUCCESSFULLY: THE THREE CASE STUDIES COMPARED

During their pre-teaching interviews all the children from the three case studies described their ideas about electricity in terms of 'power'; a majority of them specifically equated 'electricity' and 'power'. They talked about 'electricity' that was 'doing things' and 'making things go'. All of the children knew that wires were needed and they envisaged 'electricity' which was 'running through the wires' to 'do something'. None of the children had a scientific particle model for electricity. In fact, only one child had any kind of particle model. All of the children thought that the battery stored the electricity (and was the source of the 'power'), and that whatever 'ran through the wires' came from the battery.

For all three teachers a fundamental part of their objectives was that children should understand electricity as the flow of tiny particles called electrons which are already present in the wires of the circuit. This was a prominent feature of the teaching in all the case studies. In addition two of the teachers, Joan and Sarah, had objectives about the children understanding that the role of the battery is to provide the push to move the electrons (Lucy also introduced this idea although she did not specify it as one of her objectives).

To a significant extent these objectives were achieved. After teaching, for all of Joan's and Sarah's children, electrons were a notable feature of their new understanding. Five of Lucy's children had a particle model for electricity and for three of these the particles were electrons. Of the other two, one talked about 'cells' rather than electrons. This was possibly an inaccurate learning of the name for a concept rather than lack of understanding of the concept itself. The other talked about 'little bits of electricity' but gave them no name. The depth and accuracy of the understanding of electrons varied between the children but clearly electrons were a concept which had been successfully introduced and which could be built on in the future.

Both Joan and Sarah were successful in their teaching about the role of the battery. After teaching, all of their children had learnt that the battery provides the push to move the electrons. Furthermore, four of Joan's children and five of Sarah's demonstrated understanding that the electrons are already present in the wires and do not emanate from the battery.

These results are summarised in Table 9.

Table 9   Numbers of children with each understanding pre- and post-teaching

PRE-TEACHING	JOAN	LUCY	SARAH
• electricity = 'power', makes things go	6	6	6
• electricity goes through wires	6	6	6
• no particle model	5 + 1 ns	6	6
• battery is the source of / stores electricity	6	6	6
POST-TEACHING			
• electricity understood in terms of particles	6	5	6
• these particles are electrons	6	3	6
• battery pushes the electrons	6	0*	6
• electrons are already in the wires	4	0*	5

Note: total of six children for each teacher   * These ideas were not specified as learning
ns = non-scientific   objectives by Lucy

WHAT THE CHILDREN LEARNT SUCCESSFULLY: A CLOSER LOOK AT JOAN'S CHILDREN'S LEARNING

All of Joan's children had made notable strides forward in their understanding of electricity and electric circuits. Most recognised, and were able to talk knowledgeably to the researchers about, the key scientific concepts which she was trying to introduce. They were able to use these scientific concepts to explain the electrical phenomena they had experienced. There was clear evidence that many of the misconceptions which the children held pre-teaching were refuted and replaced with more scientific conceptions. The most striking areas of learning are identified below together with quotes from the interviews.

Electrons - the particulate nature of electricity
All of the children had learnt the word 'electrons' and used it in their explanations of electricity. They all embraced the idea of electrons travelling in the wires in an electric circuit. Pre-teaching, five of the children had no particle model for electricity and one had a non-scientific particle model. A key feature of many of the pre-teaching explanations equated 'power' with 'electricity':

| Interviewer: | What's electricity to you? |
| Laura: | It makes things work - the power of it makes things work .. Well, it's like a circuit - the power has to run through all of them for the bulb to light up - through the wires. |

And when describing what electricity would look like if you saw inside a wire:

| Jack: | Like a very fast blue light - like lightening. |

| Neil: | Like these sparkling things. Just like air particles, really white and like flashing. |

Post-teaching, four of the children demonstrated an understanding of the particulate nature of electricity in terms of very small moving particles called electrons:

Neil:	.. the electrons are like little particles of electric.
Interviewer:	.. How did you see it before?
Neil:	Like loads of stars all trembling.

| Darren: | .. inside the wire there are thousands of tiny electrons moving one way. |

| Jack: | In the first one (*pre-teaching*) I thought it's like a streak of light. Now I know it's like really, really tiny pieces. |

The other two children demonstrated a partial scientific understanding of the particulate nature of electricity. They understood tiny moving electrons but they also incorporated into their understanding of electrons some of their pre-teaching ideas about 'sparkly things':

| Interviewer: | How do you see electrons in your mind? |
| Lyn: | Little dots .. Well I think still about the sparkly dots and sometimes see things that are sparkly dots .. |

Electrons - in the wires already

Pre-teaching, all of the children thought that the battery was a source of electricity. They thought that whatever electricity was, it came out of the battery to the bulb (or other device in the circuit). Those who thought that electricity involved 'something' moving or 'flowing' round a circuit thought that 'something' came out of the battery and flowed along the wires. The battery 'stored' that 'something':

| Neil: | I would see at one stage the battery's totally full. Then when she connects it, the electric would be going down, like really slowly. |

| Laura: | The battery's job is to supply the power to light up the bulb (*power here equated with electricity*). |

Post-teaching, four of the children had clearly learnt correctly that the electrons exist in the wires all the time. They do not emanate from the battery. The electrons are moving randomly until the wire is connected in a circuit when they move in one direction.

Darren: (*describing how his ideas have changed*) .. because there is already electricity, electrons, in the wires ..

Neil: I thought before that the battery supplied the power, all the electric - electrons - it doesn't ..
Interviewer: So the electrons don't come from the battery?
Neil: No. They are in the wire.

The other two children had learnt about electrons in the wires but they also thought that the battery supplied electrons. These children have a partial understanding of the scientific concept: their ideas have developed to incorporate electrons but they retain the misconception about electricity emanating from the battery.

Lyn: (*describing what happens in a battery*) Trying to get out (of the battery) I think. The electrons pushing, trying to get out and then find a way out .. when they come out they are all being pushed along together .. They are all going round at the same time.

The battery pushes the electrons - why the electrons move
All the children learnt that the function of the battery is to provide the push to move the electrons. They also learnt that the voltage of a battery, which is the 'V' written on it, determines the size of the push. The bigger the voltage the larger the push.

Pre-teaching, all of the children thought that the battery was a source or store of electricity and that the voltage was the amount of power or electricity in the battery:

Helen: (*describing why the bulb lights*) .. by the battery giving the electricity to it. .. The job of the battery is to give power to the bulb to light up. .. Well, it (*the battery*) stores electricity in it and then it will go through the wires and give the bulb electricity ..

Jack: 'V' .. has a number of voltage on it which is the power strength of it that you've got to go into the light bulb.

Darren: Volts is a measurement of electricity .. in the battery .. there is more electricity (in a 6 volt battery) and the bulb gets more electricity so it shines brighter.

Post-teaching all of the children acquired the scientific idea of push:

Jack: I thought the battery held electricity before .. (and now) I know the wires have electrons in them and the battery just provides the push. ....It doesn't actually give electrons to the wire, it just pushes the ones that are already in the wire.

Helen: (*describing the battery*) .. depending on the voltage - it gives it a bigger push. .. (*referring to previous knowledge*) I didn't know the voltage was measured by the push of the battery.

Three of the children showed understanding of the link between the voltage of the battery, the push provided by the battery, the speed of the electrons and the brightness of the bulb. The bigger the voltage of the battery, then the bigger the push to move the electrons and so, for a given circuit, if the electrons experience a greater push they will move faster and the bulb will shine brighter:

Darren: .. the 1.5 volt battery has a smaller push and the electrons move slower, but with the 6 volt the push is greater and the bulb shines brighter.

The electrons are pushed by the battery in one direction

All the children learnt correctly that the battery pushes the electrons all around a circuit in one direction. Pre-teaching, four of the children held what is commonly called a clashing currents view of the electricity in a simple circuit. They thought that the electricity travelled from both ends of the battery and met, or collided, in the bulb. It was this collision which caused the bulb to light:

Jack: (*describing the movement of the electricity*) It (*the electricity*) comes from the top and the bottom and sort of meets at the bulb.

Neil: (*describing electricity through a bulb*) The electric going up these two metal bits in the bulb and joining it where I think it would collide and it would make light, like by the bang of it .. like electric against electric (*child makes movement with hands from one side and the other side - two hands coming together*) .. like a big bang like when a car crashes, like, against the front.

After teaching all of the children talked of the electrons moving in the same direction through all parts of the circuit. Included in this was their ability to describe the electrons travelling through the wire in the bulb in one direction and that the bulb lit as a result of the electrons travelling through it:

Jack: (*describing the movement of electricity in a circuit*) The battery is pushing the electrons from the top (of the battery) to the bulb, into the bulb, up the line, across the wiggly bit (*i.e. the bulb's filament*), down the other line and back through to the bottom of the battery.

The 'amount of electricity' is the same all the way round a series circuit

All the children learnt that there is the same 'amount of electricity' in all parts of a simple series circuit. They described the amount of electricity in terms of electrons moving in the wires.

Pre-teaching, there were two groups of ideas. Some children thought that the electricity met in the bulb and somehow disappeared, either fizzling out or being burnt up. This was part of the clashing currents model. When these children were first introduced to electrons they then thought that the electrons somehow disappeared in the bulb. Others thought that some of the electricity was used up in the bulb, in order to make it light, and so there would be less of it in the wire after the bulb:

Jack: I thought when the electrons got to the bulb they fizzled out.

Neil: When we first started the lesson I thought the electrons came from both sides of the battery, came along the wires, into the bulb and like burnt up.

Darren: The electricity comes out of the plus end and it goes to the bulb and then back into the bottom (of the battery). The excess electricity goes into the bottom bit, I think .. because the electricity gets used up lighting the bulb.

Jack: I thought the electricity went into the next wire sort of weaker than it went into the first wire.

The teacher introduced a meter, called an ammeter, to the children and used it to 'measure the electricity' before and after a bulb in a simple circuit. To be more precise, an ammeter measures electric current but this was not explicitly explained to the children. After teaching, the children described the same amount of electrons in the wires before and after a bulb in a series circuit and several of them explicitly refuted their previous ideas:

Laura: *(rejection of consumption model after using an ammeter)* I expected this bit coming from the battery to the .. (bulb) .. to be stronger and then on the other side to be weaker. We found that electricity was exactly the same on each side. The electrons were exactly the same.

Neil: The electrons come from one way, from the positive terminal to the negative .. the same amount all round and they all start at the same time.

Darren: Before I thought the electricity is used up in the bulb .. (but now I think) it is the same in both (wires) ..

Note that in the second quote above the child is correct about the amount of electrons but incorrectly states that they are moving from positive to negative (this reflects an error in Joan's

100

teaching - she was herself confused about current direction).

Parallel circuits - what they are, why they are better
The children all learned the procedural knowledge of how to connect up a parallel circuit. Pre-teaching, all except one child had no knowledge of parallel circuits:

Laura: *(referring to the test question on parallel circuits)* I didn't understand this .. When it says the two wires are connecting the two bulbs and battery in parallel, I didn't know that.

Post-teaching, all the children could explain the connections for a parallel circuit. Five children had learnt that a parallel circuit is better because the bulbs are brighter than in series, and four had learnt that it is better because if one bulb is removed the other stays alight. However, only two of the children could explain that a parallel circuit as made up of two (or more) independent circuits:

Laura: *(referring to parallel circuits)* It's better because the bulb shines a lot brighter in a parallel circuit than in a series. If you take one bulb out the other won't go out.

Jack: It *(a parallel circuit)* means you can light two bulbs with one battery and get a lot of light from both bulbs; when in a series circuit, with two bulbs and one battery, you won't get the light shining so bright.

COULD THE TEACHING HAVE BEEN DEVELOPED?

It is clear that all of the children did make significant leaps forward in their knowledge and understanding. However, there are some striking examples of where, with only a little more input from the teacher, it would appear that this knowledge and understanding could have been developed further. Some of these examples are described below.

The nature of electrons
All the children, as has already been described, learnt the word electrons and could use it to explain circuits. Instead of the vague word electricity they now talked with confidence about electrons moving in wires. They appeared to find it a useful idea and a powerful tool for explanations. However, they only linked electrons with electricity. It would be a relatively small step to extend the concept of electrons to that of a fundamental constituent of all matter. What is needed is the idea that all matter is made up of very, very small particles called atoms and that electrons are part of those atoms.

An electron model for conductors and insulators
All of the children developed their factual knowledge about which substances are conductors

and which insulators. However, only two explained these in terms of electrons. The idea that conductors have free electrons, that is electrons which are not strongly held to the rest of the atom, and so are able to move, and that insulators only have electrons which are strongly held to the rest of the atom and so cannot move could have been developed from a more fundamental concept of the nature of matter.

Electric current

Pre-teaching, the children either linked electric current with voltage and power, or thought of it as something flowing along a wire:

> Lyn: Electric current is when electricity runs through wires .. current is what the battery, like, the sort of power source sends out to go through the wires.

> Helen: Electric current is a flow of electricity which is measured in volts .. sort of a power ..

Post-teaching, even though they all talked about electrons, only three of the children explicitly equated electric current with the movement of electrons in the wires. There was evidence of some children incorporating electrons into their original idea which was still intact. For example:

> Helen: .. electric current is a current running through the wires making electrons move with the current.

Greater emphasis could have been placed on the description of electric current as the flow of electrons (more precisely the rate of flow of electrons). The greater the current then the greater the flow of electrons.

In addition, a more explicit distinction could have been made between current and voltage. The children clearly understood voltage as a measure of the push of the battery. The bigger the voltage the bigger the push on the electrons, and therefore, as some of the children learnt, the faster the electrons move (for a given circuit). The next step, to say the faster moving electrons are a higher current and hence higher voltage (higher push) gives higher current (faster electrons), was not made.

Current in a series circuit

The children all learnt that two bulbs in series are dimmer than one bulb alone. The reasons for this in terms of the current were not explored. The concept of resistance (how easily electrons can flow through something) was not introduced and so the opportunity was not taken to explore how adding bulbs in a circuit increases the resistance and hence decreases the current.

Particle model for bulb lighting

The children rejected their previous explanations for why the bulb lit but were offered no alternatives and some were puzzled about what was happening inside the bulb. If the concept of resistance had been introduced then the bulb could have been described as containing a short piece of high resistance wire. As the electrons pass through the bulb they collide with the fixed atoms in the resistance wire. It is these collisions which produce the light.

Electron direction

The children all correctly learnt that the electrons flow around the circuit in one direction but they were incorrectly taught this direction as from the positive terminal of the battery to the negative. This is the direction of the 'conventional current' whereas the electrons flow from negative to positive (see Appendix VII). This clearly is a source of difficulty and, at this level, it could be argued that as long as the flow is understood to be unidirectional the accuracy of the direction does not matter.

Function of the ammeter

The teacher very successfully introduced an ammeter to refute the children's idea that the electricity was used up inside the bulb. The children were convinced that there was the same amount of electricity before and after the bulb. Unfortunately, what the ammeter was measuring was not made clear. The children all described it as measuring the volts. This further emphasises the need to make explicit and clear the distinction between voltage and current and to explain the ammeter as a device for measuring current, or the rate of electrons passing through a slice of wire, at different places in a circuit. The ammeter also could have been used to explore the current in a series circuit with one and then two bulbs.

CHILDREN'S REASONS FOR THEIR LEARNING

The children were asked at various stages in the interviews what they thought had helped them learn. The following were the most commonly mentioned things.

Bicycle chain analogy

In this analogy a simple circuit is likened to a bicycle chain. The push on the pedals is analogous to the push from the battery and the links on the chain are analogous to the electrons. The teacher had brought a bike into the classroom and had made extensive reference to the analogy. All the children except one made frequent references to this analogy. It had helped them visualise the electrons moving in a circuit and in particular had helped them understand the unidirectional flow and the amount of electricity being the same at all points in the circuit.

Activities

All of the children made some reference to them 'doing' - either doing experiments or making circuits or seeing for themselves something happen.

Teacher talking / explaining

All of the children made reference to the teacher explaining. In particular, the diagrams the teacher had drawn of electrons in a wire had made an impact on the children.

Children talk / discussion

The teacher had made extensive use of discussions and had encouraged the children to share their ideas and explanations. Five of the children commented that these discussions had helped them clarify their ideas.

SUMMARY

This chapter has focused on the children's learning of some of the important concepts which the teachers had in their objectives for their lessons. The six children from each case study who were interviewed had all developed their understanding to some extent and many of the children had made considerable advances in their understanding.

The concept of electrons was central to the teaching in all three case studies and, after teaching, fifteen out of the eighteen children discussed electricity and electric circuits in terms of electrons.

Where it was taught as an objective, in two of the case studies, the role of the battery as the 'pusher' of the electrons was effectively learnt by all of the children.

Although significant learning did take place there were a number of instances when with only a little more, or slightly different, input from the teacher the learning could possibly have been greater. Examples of these have been identified in the case of one teacher, Joan.

CHAPTER 7

EFFECTIVE TEACHING

This final chapter returns to the definition of effective teaching adopted at the outset of this project, and considers the preparation of the teachers for participation in the research and the effectiveness of the teaching observed. It goes on to discuss the role of subject knowledge in effective teaching and insights gained into the nature of teaching knowledge both for electricity in particular and more generally. In a final section, the principal outcomes of the research are summarised briefly.

WHAT IS EFFECTIVE TEACHING?

The view taken during the study

Judgments about what constitutes effective teaching may be based upon teachers' own perceptions of their performance, the perception of their colleagues or pupils, or examination and test results. The present research judged effective teaching in terms of learning outcomes, and in particular the ways in which pupils' understanding of the ideas taught had changed following teaching.

Pupils' understanding of the ideas to be taught were appraised before and after teaching using a pencil and paper test given to each whole class and tailored to the objectives specified in advance by each teacher. Also, six pupils from each class were interviewed in depth before and after teaching so that their understanding of these same ideas could be gauged with considerable confidence. The pencil and paper test scores of the interviewed pupils were checked against their interview scores to assess the validity of the test as a measure of understanding (see Appendix IV). This procedure showed that the scores from the pencil and paper tests tended to underestimate children's understanding.

The mean test score for the whole class for a given objective was used as an indicator of the effectiveness of the teaching for that objective, recognising that test scores were likely to have underestimated the learning achieved.

PREPARATION FOR EFFECTIVE TEACHING

The inservice training

Prior to the research project, all the teachers lacked confidence in teaching electricity - one (Joan) avoided it if at all possible. They admitted to a personal lack of knowledge and understanding of electricity and restricted the scope of their work with children to descriptions of phenomena and practice of procedural skills. The teaching did not attempt to deal with the concepts necessary to *understand* the behaviour of electric circuits.

In order to shift the emphasis in the approach used by these teachers towards developing children's understanding of concepts, the INSET described in Chapter 2 was provided. The purpose of this was to:

- develop teachers' own personal understanding of concepts to do with electricity and circuits i.e. improve their subject knowledge.

- introduce a range of perspectives on science teaching in general and the teaching of electricity in particular, which the teachers could use as a model for their own teaching i.e. develop their teaching knowledge.

- help teachers think about the *concepts* they want children to understand as a result of their teaching.

- help teachers gain confidence in their ability to teach electricity.

Other key facets of the training were an emphasis on active experience (both practically and intellectually active); plenty of discussion and posing of challenging questions about electricity and circuits; the use of analogies and models to promote understanding; and the fostering of a relaxed and sociable environment to help build trust and confidence. The teachers were introduced to typical misconceptions that research has shown children often hold about electricity and simple circuits, and to a model of teaching which emphasises the importance of eliciting, challenging and developing these prior ideas.

These techniques resulted in the teachers achieving significant learning of new knowledge which they looked forward to trying out in their classrooms.

An important finding of the subsequent research was that the teachers transferred ideas and strategies from the INSET, which was aimed at themselves as adult learners, directly into the classroom and often used them virtually unmodified with pupils. They clearly found these approaches helpful in developing their own understanding, and judged the techniques to be appropriate for children as well. With hindsight, this can be recognised as almost inevitable. The degree of subject knowledge that can be developed in three days (or even much longer?) is insufficient for the teachers to develop their own teaching knowledge with any confidence. Perhaps of necessity, they used the approaches and analogies devised by experts and which had worked with themselves as learners.

Hence we believe it to be important that, when developing materials for primary science teacher education, the approaches used should be such that they can be transferred directly to the classroom.

The concepts introduced

The basic concepts covered in the inservice training are listed in Table 2 of Chapter 2. An important feature of the approach taken is that it is based on a *particulate* view of the nature of electricity i.e. electricity consists of particles called electrons. When these particles are made to move in the same direction, they form an electric current. The role of the battery in a circuit is to provide the push to move the electrons.

This approach to the teaching of electricity is not commonly found in primary science publications. If current is mentioned, it is rarely identified with moving electrons. Some texts regard electricity as energy - an approach which is problematic given the difficulty of the energy concept (but see the further comments below). Few texts identify the battery as providing the push in a circuit.

A second important finding of the research is that both teachers and pupils readily accept and make use of a particulate view of electricity. Electricity as electrons, current as moving electrons, and the role of the battery as providing the push to move the electrons are ideas which can form the basis of a more conceptual approach to the teaching of electricity at primary level.

However, despite the success of this particulate approach, there was considerable evidence that children cling strongly to an intuitive view that something is used up in the circuit. This notion is of course correct, but it is energy which is consumed (or more strictly speaking, transferred from battery to bulb) not current.

While teachers in these case studies did recognise that current (moving electrons) is not used up, they failed to build on the children's intuitive notion and identify the bulb as an energy 'consumer'. So we are left to wonder about the mental models the children now have for a bulb lighting given the ready acceptance that electrons are not consumed.

In the view of the research team, even introductory teaching needs to make the distinction between current conservation and energy consumption (transfer) explicit, perhaps by making use of the sweet chain analogy (Appendix VI) or the elaboration of the bicycle chain analogy given on page 36. This does not require any teaching about energy - simply using the name energy in these two analogies is a step in the right direction.

On reflection, the inservice training did not sufficiently emphasise the distinction between current conservation and energy 'consumption'. Later in this chapter we develop the view of teaching knowledge described in Chapter 1 to include knowledge of what to emphasise. The current-energy distinction is one example of this.

As a final point here we wish to point out that some texts for primary schools identify the word electricity with both energy (batteries are *sources* of electricity) and, at other places in the same publication, with current (electricity *flows* round a circuit). This, we suggest, is the worst of all worlds and can cause considerable confusion.

HOW EFFECTIVE WERE THE TEACHERS?

An objective appraisal - the researchers' viewpoint

Tables 3, 6 and 7 show the pre- and post-teaching mean scores of the three classes on a scale from 0 (little or no understanding) through 1 (some understanding) to 2 (good understanding). Inspection of these shows that for all 29 objectives taught, improvement had occurred following teaching. The degree of improvement varied:

- in Joan's case, scores increased by 1.00 or more in seven out of her nine objectives. With Lucy's six objectives, the largest increase seen between pre- and post-teaching mean scores was 0.95, while for Sarah's fourteen objectives it was 0.88.

- with Joan's objectives there was an average increase of 1.07 from pre- to post-teaching mean scores. For both Lucy and Sarah this average increase was 0.55.

- the range and scope of Sarah's fourteen objectives was far greater than Lucy's six so, although the average increase in scores was the same, this represented a greater amount of learning by Sarah's children.

The in-depth interviews with the sub-group of six children from each class described in Chapter 6 provide insights into the scope and limitations of the knowledge and understanding achieved. Table 9 in that chapter summarises some of the learning gains. Each teacher had some effect in developing their children's understanding of the ideas taught. In some cases (and especially in the case of Joan), the improvement in understanding of ideas not usually taught to this age group was quite remarkable.

Teachers' own views about their performance

Post-teaching, the teachers were asked for their reflections on their successes and difficulties, the appropriateness of their objectives, the role children's misconceptions played in their teaching, and any other points that arose.

With regard to the children's attainment, Joan felt (correctly) that most of her children had acquired the concepts expressed in her objectives. Lucy thought, over-optimistically, that most children had grasped four of her six objectives but was too pessimistic in her view that two others had not been understood. Sarah was rightly doubtful about children's understanding of some objectives and her judgment of the success achieved with others was rather optimistic.

Among the successes achieved all three teachers cited the children's enjoyment of the sessions and, particularly in Lucy's case, described insights into their practice which they had gained from this first attempt at teaching electricity in this way. Joan and Sarah's successes also included an increased level of confidence in their personal subject knowledge, children's use of, and familiarity with, the equipment, and the effectiveness of the planned overall approach. Lucy felt she had effectively improved children's use of scientific language.

Difficulties described by all three teachers' were their own understanding of certain concepts i.e. aspects of their subject knowledge, technological problems with equipment, the constraints of time, worries about children's questioning leading beyond the bounds of their subject knowledge and a persisting insecurity with respect to some concepts (Joan and Lucy talked about being only one step ahead of the children with some ideas). Both Joan and Sarah thought that restricting the scope of the sessions only to those ideas about electricity with which they felt comfortable was a factor which made their teaching more effective.

Views about the match between the cognitive level of the objectives set and the children's abilities varied. Initially Joan worried that her objectives were aimed 'too low' but found from her investigation of the children's prior ideas that these fears were unfounded. Lucy thought that her objectives aimed too high and she should have kept things simpler. Sarah felt that her objectives were appropriate for 11 year olds and that indeed they could be 'pushed on more', but admitted that this was a subjective feeling not based on evidence of children's learning.

What were the teachers' perceptions of the role children's misconceptions played in their teaching? Joan felt that she had difficulty knowing where her children were starting from, conceptually speaking, but the training had convinced her that finding this out was something she 'really ought to do' (and which she did do very successfully). Lucy admitted that she did not know what the children's existing ideas were, but eliciting these received little attention in her teaching. Sarah, when asked about the role of children's misconceptions in her teaching, seemed to misunderstand the question. She talked about ideas in the lessons which may have been incorrectly understood and the revision quiz provided at the end of the teaching sequence in which any of these errors in understanding could be addressed. As with Lucy, elicitation of children's existing prior ideas played little part in her actual teaching.

Among other issues mentioned was the INSET. Joan felt that the INSET materials had strongly influenced her to use children's prior ideas as her starting point i.e. they affected her teaching knowledge. Sarah felt the INSET had influenced only her subject knowledge but in this she was mistaken since both she and Joan made extensive use of the analogies presented in the materials which are, of course, a key aspect of teaching knowledge.

So the teachers' subjective judgments about the effect of their teaching frequently did not correspond to those derived from more objective test data. However, their perceptions showed areas of both satisfaction and concern about their efforts to implement the model for effective teaching provided during their training.

THE ROLE OF SUBJECT KNOWLEDGE

Why it is necessary

It is self-evident that possession of adequate subject knowledge is necessary for the teacher who wishes to address children's understanding, for how can learners be led along a path of conceptual development unless the guide has knowledge of the eventual destination and of the pitfalls that lie in wait along the road?

Children do not somehow 'discover' ideas about electricity that correspond to those of the scientist, and which are often counter-intuitive, simply by experimenting with equipment in the classroom. Such a naive inductivist view equates the exploratory activities of the pupil with the efforts of great minds of the past. The models and constructs that scientists have developed, such as the electron, voltage, current and so on, need to be understood by the teacher so that they can be presented to children in a way which is appropriate to their level of development.

What is appropriate subject knowledge for primary school teachers?

During the INSET teachers did not seem to encounter any ideas about electricity beyond their capabilities. The subject knowledge they acquired from the training was presented in a non-quantitative way making extensive use of analogies and strongly visual comparisons. Some ideas were more easily acquired than others but teachers did cope with the subject knowledge presented.

Some teachers remarked on their 'ephemeral understanding' where an idea would be seemingly clear to them at one moment but would then flit away and be lost the next. Teachers' awareness of how variable their hold was on different ideas prompted some to restrict the planned scope of their teaching to those ideas with which they felt secure. In this way the limitations of their subject knowledge exercised control over what was taught to the children. The problem is that discussions with children can lead into areas of subject knowledge beyond those planned - and teachers expressed their worries about this - so the range of subject knowledge a teacher needs in order to feel secure will exceed that which is to be taught to the children. Where are the boundaries to be drawn for primary school teachers?

It has been suggested that primary teachers' subject knowledge should correspond to that required at Level 8 of the National Curriculum, perhaps so that they will be able to teach the bright 11 year old at Level 6. Our own view is that this is not the most helpful or realistic way of thinking about subject knowledge. So, for example, Level 8 knowledge may be more quantitative and introduce additional concepts which are not directly relevant to Key Stages 1 and 2. What teachers need is a deep, qualitative understanding of the ideas they *do* have to teach. In the inservice training on electricity and circuits provided for this research, the qualitative depth of treatment and intellectual challenge were far greater than that of a GCSE course, but the scope was considerably less.

The evidence from this research is that teachers seemed to be comfortable with the view of electricity seen in terms of electrons which is adopted in this book and judged that it was also appropriate for their children. The results for children's attainment described earlier show that this judgment was not unreasonable.

In our view the ideas taught to the teachers during their INSET provided a sound and adequate basis for the teaching of ideas about electricity, which are rather more advanced than those hitherto regarded as appropriate, to pupils at the upper end of the primary school.

However, having adequate subject knowledge is clearly, for a teacher, only a first step. The professional task is to help children acquire this knowledge and this research has cast new light on the teaching knowledge which is needed to achieve this.

THE NATURE OF TEACHING KNOWLEDGE: AN EXPANDED VIEW

Knowing how to make ideas accessible to children - called pedagogical content knowledge in the academic literature - is referred to in this book, more simply, as teaching knowledge. In Chapter 1 we put forward Shulman's view that this includes knowledge of:

- the conceptions and preconceptions that children of different ages and backgrounds bring with them to the learning of a topic.

- the strategies most likely to be fruitful in reorganising the understanding of learners.

  [Where we now stress that, in the case of science, this includes knowledge of relevant practical activities, experiments and equipment to use.]

- the usual forms of representation of ideas, the most powerful analogies, illustrations, examples, explanations and demonstrations.

The goal of this research has been to identify the teacher subject and teaching knowledge which can help children develop effectively their understanding of electricity and simple circuits. In pursuit of this goal, our view of teaching knowledge has expanded to include these other aspects:

- knowledge of appropriate language and scientific terms to use with children.

- knowledge of how to simplify validly what are often very sophisticated ideas - for example, describing the voltage of a battery as the amount of push exerted on the electrons in a circuit.

  With regard to this point, it is clear that one person's subject knowledge is another's teaching knowledge. So, for example, the various simplified ideas about electricity presented to the teachers during the INSET became their subject knowledge. For the expert physicist, these simplified viewpoints constitute teaching knowledge derived from a much deeper understanding of electricity which makes up his or her subject knowledge (see Commentary, Chapter 3).

- knowledge of what to emphasise. In the present research the teachers were anxious to explain and emphasise what they understood to be the scientific view. But, in our view, of equal importance is appropriate emphasis on what is *not* the scientific view. This links most obviously to children's misconceptions and the need to continuously revisit and emphasise what is *not* the case e.g. the battery is not the source of the current, and a bulb does not use up current.

- simple technological knowledge of equipment. All three teachers in this research experienced difficulties arising from a lack of technical knowledge e.g. mixing components such as bulbs, buzzers and motors designed to work with different battery voltages. A further important example is the failure of nominally identical bulbs to shine with the same brightness in a series circuit. This latter problem can be baffling for an inexperienced teacher, yet is a technical problem which can easily be overcome (see Appendix V of our book *Current Understanding*).

TEACHING KNOWLEDGE FOR ELECTRICITY

Here we summarise aspects of teaching knowledge for teaching electricity which have emerged from the research and describe the use made of them by the three teachers.

Using children's prior ideas

The teachers' perceptions of the role played by children's misconception in their teaching have been described earlier. The authors' view is that of the three teachers, Joan's pedagogy was the most geared towards eliciting children's prior ideas and then trying to modify them towards the scientific view - it contained a great deal of focused discussion leading to testing of their ideas. The children's misconceptions were challenged by investigation which was both physically and intellectually active. Lucy's teaching did not attempt to develop children's existing ideas and featured much less discussion. Sarah allowed for the presence of a well-known children's misconception (the *consumption model* for current - Fig 7b) and planned a circus activity which would refute it, if present. With this exception, her discussions aimed more at explanation of the new ideas being introduced than at modification of children's existing ideas.

Of course, eliciting and discussing 6 children's views, as Joan did, is much easier than doing so with 16 children (Sarah) or 27 (Lucy). Nevertheless, this aspect of teaching knowledge underpinned Joan's approach whereas with Sarah it was more limited and in Lucy's case only brief lip-service was paid to it. The emphasis for Joan and Lucy was more on using strategies for conveying aspects of subject knowledge to the children than on ways of finding out and challenging the children's existing views. In Lucy's case this meant that she spent much time teaching an idea that most of her pupils already had grasped - time that could have been more fruitfully spent dealing with the new ideas she was trying to introduce.

Using appropriate analogies

All three teachers made use of the bicycle chain analogy and for Joan it seemed particularly effective. This may have been because she:

- actually had a bicycle upturned on a table in the room.
- focussed in more depth on the correspondences between aspects of the analogical situation and features of the idea she was introducing (e.g. pedals = battery etc).
- involved the children more closely in the details of the analogy - for example, by getting them to draw it and producing her own visual aid when teaching.
- encouraged more participation by the children in the analogy - for example, by asking them to develop the correspondences observed rather than telling them.

Sarah also had a bicycle in the room but her teaching was more didactic than Joan's. Sarah also made use of water-in-a-pipe analogies from the INSET materials; these were not as effective as the bicycle chain, perhaps because:

- they were not presented in 'concrete' fashion (drawn representations were used).
- they involve a domain (liquid flowing through tubes) which is less familiar to children and not so relevant to their everyday experience.
- children were passive as they were taught. There is probably much scope for devising active analogies, such as the 'pupil and sweets chain' analogy (see Appendix VI), to convey ideas to children about electrons in circuits - for example, the idea of free electrons (see Commentary, Chapter 5) which was only partially understood as a result of Sarah's clear and oft-repeated, but purely verbal, explanation.
- Sarah used two analogies to illustrate an idea and her moving rapidly from one to the other may have caused confusion. It is perhaps better to deal with a single analogous situation at a time and proceed at a rate that enables children to fully take in the points being made.

Lucy referred to the bicycle chain analogy only verbally and very briefly but, unlike Joan and

Sarah, she did use the 'marbles in a jar' analogy for electric current. This has many limitations which she failed to point out. It is probable that discussion of where an analogy fails to correspond to the situation being taught can be almost as effective as discussing resemblances.

What became apparent from testing following teaching was that the analogies were effective at different levels for different individual children - some retained the details of the correspondences described while others remembered only points of more general (though still valid) resemblance between the analogical and scientific situations.

Careful use of language
All three teachers used scientific terminology; Sarah particularly showed great skill and empathy with the children in her choice of everyday words to facilitate explanations. All were aware of the dangers of loose usage such as referring to the 'size' of the battery (physical size or voltage?) and sometimes unwarranted assumptions were made about children's understanding of scientific terms, e.g. 'series' in the case of Lucy.

Another aspect of this, particularly noticeable in Lucy's case, was the need for clarity and greater precision when giving instructions and explanations.

Emphasis
Recapitulation of the content of a session at the end, and of ideas covered previously at the start of each new session is good practice which Joan and Sarah used particularly effectively. This kind of emphasis is part of general teaching knowledge.

However, as described in the example earlier, the importance of more specific emphasis often became apparent from the effects of its omission. Evidence of partial or absent understanding in some children showed the importance of emphasising key points in order to teach effectively. For example, some ambiguity in children's post-teaching views about the relationship between current and electrons was perhaps due to the teachers not emphasising sufficiently that the current *consists of moving electrons*. In another example involving two explanations for a single phenomenon, the absence of emphasis that bulb brightness depends on the size of the current, as well as that of the voltage, probably accounted for children's lack of understanding of the former.

All three teachers emphasised the idea of electrons by means of repetition and Joan and Sarah in particular stressed their presence all around the circuit by referring to the bicycle chain analogy. In spite of this the misconception that the battery supplies electrons was still present; perhaps emphasising that an incorrect idea like this is *not* the case is as important as stressing what the scientist believes *is* happening.

Technological considerations

Familiarity with possible problems with the equipment used was seen to be an important part of teaching knowledge for electricity. Knowledge of what will happen when incorrect connections are made is as important as knowing the right procedures. Lucy's problems with her children's use of the ammeter were an illustration of this.

It also became apparent that giving children equipment to use without checking in advance that it works correctly or performs the task intended was ineffective - Joan, for example, convinced her children (unintentionally) that tap water was an insulator since the 1.5 V cell she provided for the children to test its conductivity did not produce a large enough current through the water to light a bulb. If she had performed the test beforehand she would have realised that a 6 V battery was needed to provide an adequate current.

When experiments 'don't work' for these kinds of reasons, an informed explanation by the teacher followed by a successful modification can give even deeper insights than if it 'works' first time, but lacking this, credibility can be lost which makes the teaching ineffective.

Other aspects of the use of equipment which contributed to more effective teaching became apparent. Reassuring children at the start that the equipment was safe to use was good practice which built confidence. Making available only those items of equipment that are needed for the investigation in hand made both Joan and Sarah's teaching more effective. Lucy learned this lesson the hard way - because so much equipment was provided for the children, too much of their activity consisted of random exploration rather than directed, structured investigation.

FURTHER POINTS ABOUT THE TEACHING OBSERVED

In the previous paragraphs we have outlined some features of subject specific teaching knowledge which were significant in this research programme. However, there were a number of further aspects of the teaching which, in the view of the research team, certainly contributed to effectiveness. Whether or not these are regarded as subject specific teaching knowledge depends, perhaps, on how widely one wishes to interpret this term. Leaving this issue aside, the following points about the teaching observed were also apparent:

- controlling the content

  The teachers' control of the scope of sessions by restricting their teaching to those aspects of subject knowledge with which they felt comfortable (and which could be dealt with in the time available) seems to have been effective. This of course requires careful and thorough planning. Some ideas which teachers chose to teach, such as the relationship between current direction and the working of one-way conducting devices (e.g. a buzzer), seemed difficult for children to understand. The ineffective teaching of these ideas may have been due partly to their intrinsic difficulty but also to inadequate teaching knowledge.

115

- getting the right mix.

It was evident that there was a place both for presenting children with ready-made scientific explanations and asking them to make their own interpretations, speculations and predictions. Sarah at times over-emphasised the former and Lucy the latter. Joan seemed to achieve the most effective balance of these.

- conceptual focus.

All three teachers focused their teaching on the conceptual objectives which they had begun to plan in Session 3 of the INSET. The research team helped them to express the ideas they wanted their children to master as clearly and unambiguously as possible.

- progressive development of ideas.

Joan in particular showed how this can be done effectively by developing an existing idea which children have - for example, the circuit as a pathway - and introducing a fresh concept such as the electron as an explanatory tool. Matching the already familiar with the new, as Lucy did when teaching circuit diagrams, or extending the familiar into a new context, like Sarah extending the pathway idea to include bulb- and battery-holders, is also effective. However, teaching logically sequential ideas in the wrong order, as Sarah did with some of her circus activities, might have detracted from the effectiveness of her teaching.

- use of visual aids.

The use of teachers' own visual aids for abstract ideas, e.g. Joan's portrayal of electrons as 'dots' within the wire, seemed to be more effective than merely verbal description, as used by Sarah and Lucy. Published worksheets used, like those of Lucy, were of little relevance to ideas about electrons and could have been modified to be more effective.

- using a variety of approaches and contexts

The effectiveness of this was seen, for example, in Lucy's effective teaching of circuit diagrams where she used six approaches involving interpretation, matching tasks, handouts, equipment, explanations and board work (see Chapter 4).

- linking experiences and discussion closely

To gain maximum effectiveness from an activity, it is best not to lose the immediacy of the experience if possible - the circus approach was an efficient class management technique but it can make demands on children's recall which may lessen the effectiveness of the teaching.

- making new ideas relevant

All three teachers tried to engage the children's interest by making the concepts relevant to their experience and daily work. They did this by linking their teaching of electricity to children's work from other areas of the curriculum.

- timing of sessions

All three teachers were under pressure from the demands of the research and worried how best to fit the sessions into both the class timetable and that of the school. Lucy had to take into account another class teacher's timetable as well as her own and that of the head teacher who was covering for her.

These pressures meant that timing was not always of the teacher's choice. Lucy, for example, ran short of time (unavoidably) for one of her three sessions and this obviously decreased her effectiveness. All teachers said that they would take more time to teach the sequence on the next occasion, although Joan did feel that the 'intensity' of her four sessions had contributed to their effectiveness. Sarah's teaching sequence (five sessions) was the longest and the excessive time she devoted to some of her lessons probably decreased their effectiveness.

A FINAL POINT

During the research programme described in the previous chapters, perhaps the most noticeable quality observed in the teachers who took part was their degree of commitment. It became obvious that the teachers above all wanted to *understand* so that they could more effectively help the children in their care. In order to achieve this they were prepared to expose their own insecurity and to be scrutinised in detail by outsiders as they attempted to teach in a new way. The teachers' courage in doing this and their readiness to discuss frankly their ideas and their performance earned the admiration, gratitude and respect of the research team.

SUMMARY

In summary, the main outcomes of this research were as follows:

- identification of a set of concepts in electricity which can be taught effectively to both primary school teachers and pupils. These concepts are not widely introduced in primary school science publications yet, from the evidence of the research, are readily accessible to teachers and pupils and could form a fruitful basis for a more conceptual approach to this topic in primary schools.

- identification, and elaboration through case studies and expert commentary, of teaching knowledge which can be effective in developing these concepts.

- development of an expanded view of the nature of teaching knowledge.

- the need for experts to help identify appropriate teaching knowledge, the evidence being that teachers cannot be expected to do this for themselves.

- identification of a number of further aspects of the observed teaching which seemed to contribute to effectiveness.

In addition, through the many examples and appendices dealing with subject and teaching knowledge, this book provides a wealth of material for use in the teaching of this area of the science curriculum in primary schools.

REFERENCES

Shulman, L. (1986) Those who understand: knowledge growth in teaching, *Educational Researcher*, February.

Summers, M., Kruger, C. and Mant, J. (1995) *Current Understanding: electricity concepts and practice for primary and non-specialist secondary teacher education* (Oxford University in association with the Institution of Electrical Engineers and the Understanding Electricity Educational Service).

APPENDICES

120

APPENDIX I

A COMPLETE PENCIL AND PAPER TEST
(for Joan's children)

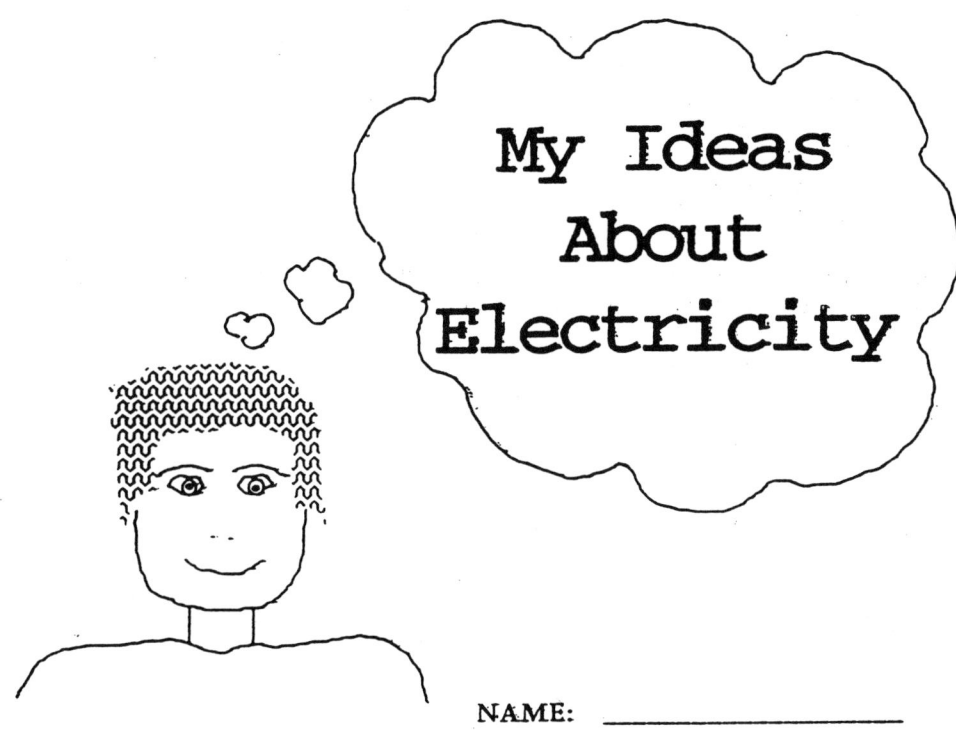

NAME: _____

On these pages you will see some drawings with questions about them.

This is <u>not a test</u> so don't worry about your answer being right or wrong.

We are very interested in <u>your own ideas</u> about what is happening in the pictures so don't talk to your friends about your answers.

If you are not sure what to do, ask your teacher for help.

PART A

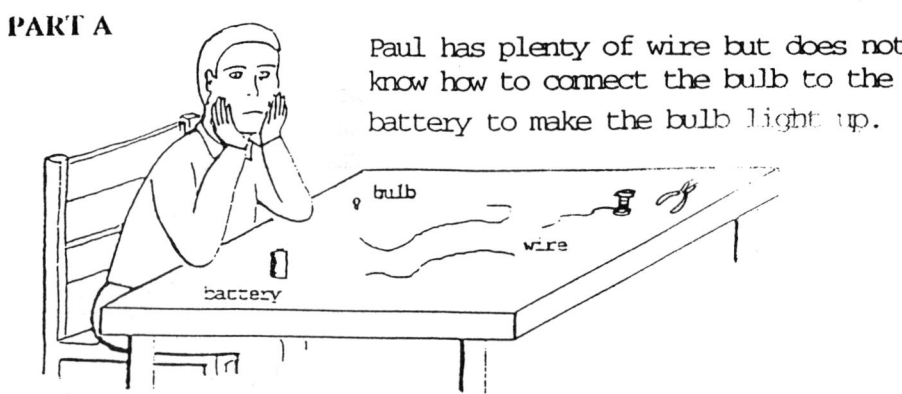

Paul has plenty of wire but does not know how to connect the bulb to the battery to make the bulb light up.

Draw very carefully how to connect the bulb and battery so that Paul would clearly understand how to make the bulb light.

A/BB

Explain your drawing here

```
┌─────────────────────────────────────────────────────────────┐
│                                                             │
│                                                             │
│                                                             │
│                                                             │
└─────────────────────────────────────────────────────────────┘
```

Now draw carefully how to connect this bulb and battery, which are in holders, so that Paul would clearly understand how to make the bulb light.

A/BBH

Explain your drawing here

```
┌─────────────────────────────────────────────────────────────┐
│                                                             │
│                                                             │
│                                                             │
│                                                             │
└─────────────────────────────────────────────────────────────┘
```

WHEN YOU HAVE FINISHED, GIVE THIS TO YOUR TEACHER AND ASK FOR PART B

APPENDIX I

A COMPLETE PENCIL AND PAPER TEST (contd)

PART B   YOUR NAME _____

This shows Burt Battery, Wally Wire, William Wire and Brenda Bulb talking to each other on the science shelf while the teacher reads to the class. Imagine that they are telling each other what job they did when they were connected together to make Brenda shine during the science lesson.

Write in each 'speech bubble' what you think they would say to each other.

Tony and Jane are talking about the meaning of the word 'current'.

Have you heard of 'electric current'?   YES ☐   NO ☐

If you have heard of it, explain what you mean by 'electric current.

Electric current is ...

B/C

The teacher has given Debbie 2 batteries to use.
Debbie has connected up her circuit using
this 1.5 V battery and the
bulb is glowing.

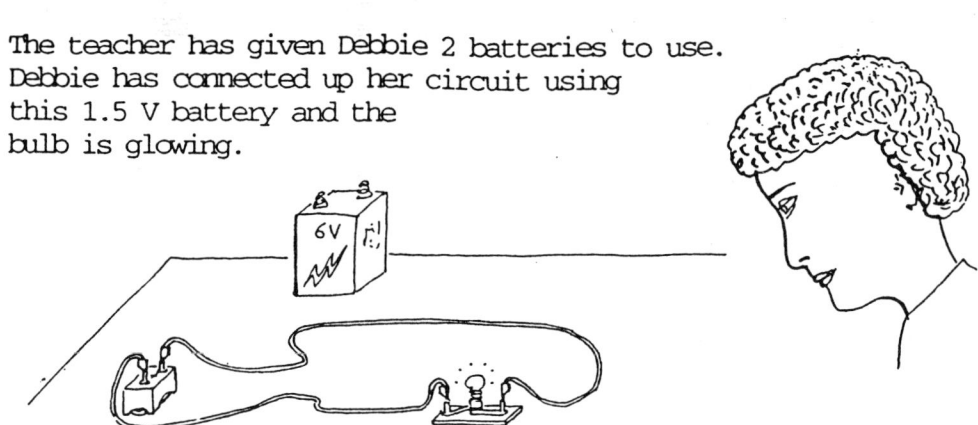

When she swaps batteries and uses the 6 V battery, the bulb
shines much more brightly.

Write down the ideas you have about '1.5 V' and '6 V' to explain
why this happens.

My explanation:

B/V

When you have done this, go to the next page

APPENDIX I

A COMPLETE PENCIL AND PAPER TEST (contd)

Julie is looking at different parts of the circuit on the table. Imagine that she wears 'X-ray mega-magnifying superspecs' which let her see what is happening deep inside things.

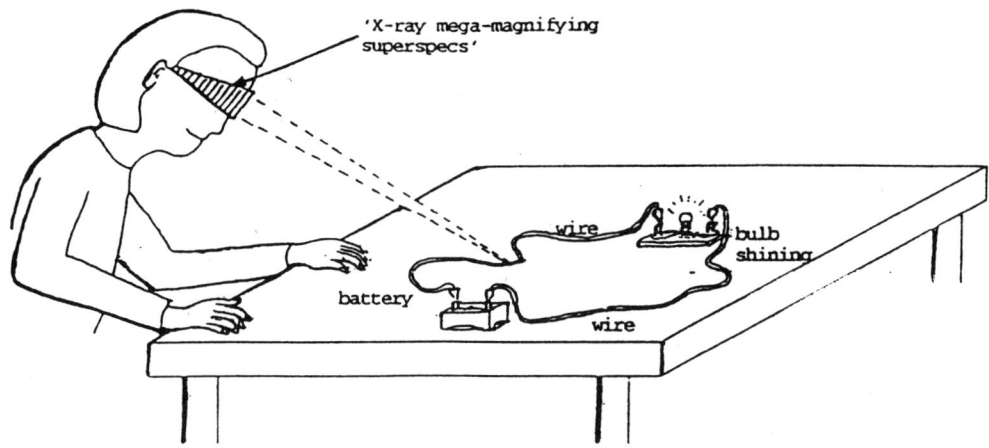

Write what you think Julie would see ...

1. ... happening inside the wire

2. ... happening inside the bulb

3. ... happening inside the battery

B/1C

125

Greg has connected up his circuit and the bulb is shining brightly.

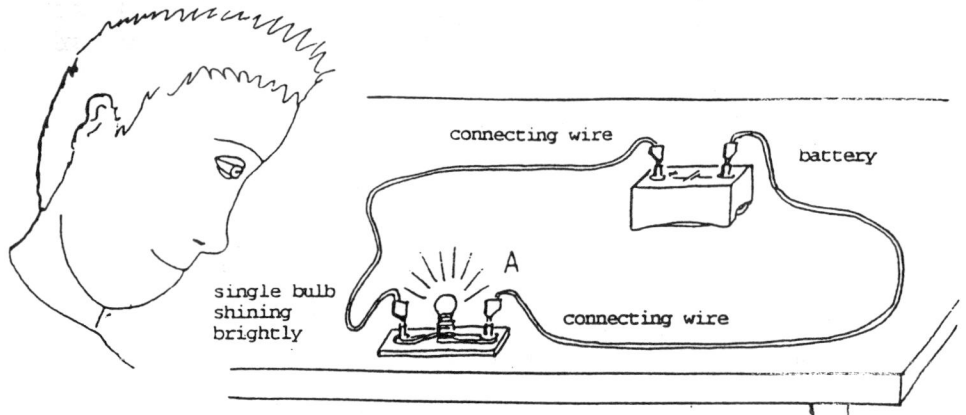

Here he is just going to connect another bulb (exactly the same) in line with the first one.

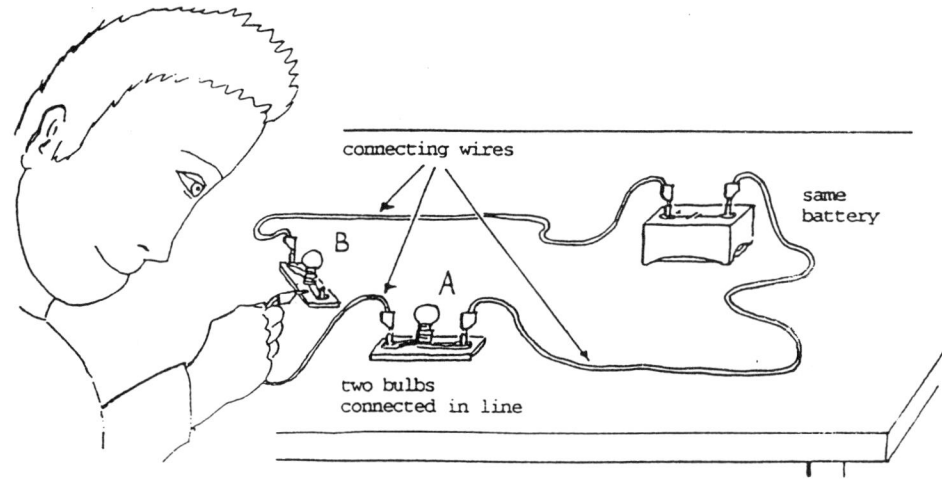

In the space below, write what you think will happen to each bulb when Greg makes the connection. Try to explain why.

I think ...

B/BIS

126

APPENDIX I

A COMPLETE PENCIL AND PAPER TEST (contd)

Henry is testing different things to see if the bulb lights.
He puts one of the things (e.g. a plastic ruler) between the two wires and touches it with the wires.
He then looks at the bulb to see if it lights.
When he does this with some things the bulb <u>does</u> light, but with other things it <u>does not</u> light.

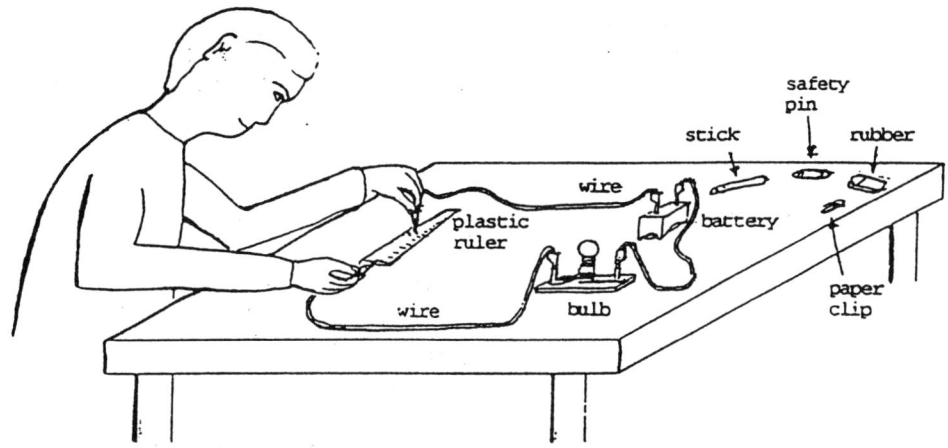

Tick YES or NO for the things on the table to show if the bulb lights or not.

stick	YES	paper clip	YES	rubber	YES	safety pin	YES
	NO		NO		NO		NO

Write 2 other things you could put between the wires (i) to make the bulb light (ii) for which the bulb would <u>not</u> light.

(i) would make the
    bulb light

(ii) would <u>not</u> make
     the bulb light

Why does the bulb light with some things but not with others?

Write in the box below why you think this happens

I think that the bulb lights with some things and not with others because ...

B/CI

127

Susan is pointing towards something which the teacher says she can connect to a battery...

It's called 'a LED' for short, Susan

Have you ever seen or heard of one of these? ☐ YES   ☐ NO

If you ticked NO, stop here and go on to the next sheet.

If you ticked YES, write down the third word in the name
    CLUE: IT BEGINS WITH D (Light Emitting D_____)

What does a LED do?   **Write your ideas in the box below** .

I think that a LED ...

What happens if you connect a LED to a battery (1) and then change the connections around (2)?

1   2

Say what you think happens

I think...

What does this tell you about the LED?

This tells me that...

B/D

APPENDIX I

A COMPLETE PENCIL AND PAPER TEST (contd)

Kevin has given his model ship 2 signal lights.
He used two bulbs, a battery and three wires, just like Greg did.

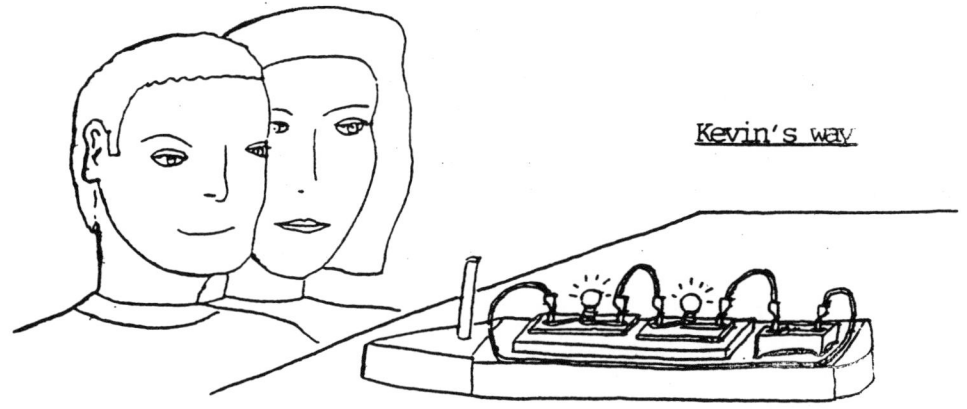

Kevin's way

Jill says a better way of connecting the 2 bulbs to the battery is
in parallel.

**Show Jill's connections (in parallel) between the bulbs and battery on this boat.
(just draw a line to stand for each wire)**

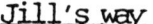

Jill's way

Say why Jill's way of connecting them is better than Kevin's.

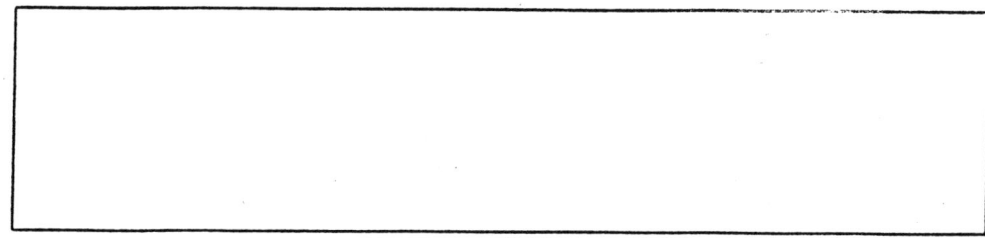

3/PB

129

The teacher has asked Zainab to say which diagram on the display board shows how the circuit on her buggy is connected.

Put what you think Zainab says (A, B, C, D, E or F) here ⎯⎯⎯⎯⎯

Explain why you chose that diagram:

I chose diagram ☐ because ...

130

APPENDIX I

A COMPLETE PENCIL AND PAPER TEST (contd)

Tony and Jane have watched their teacher connect these things together. They recognise the battery, bulb and wires but are puzzled by the other object. Can you help them?

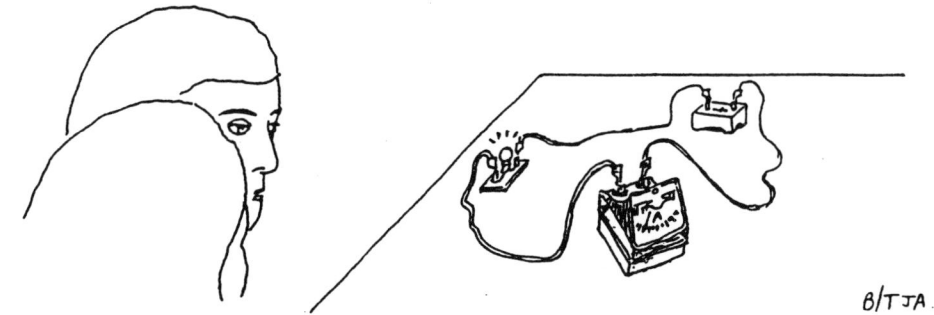

Explain what the puzzling object is and (if you can) what it's used for.

APPENDIX II

SCORING PROCEDURES AND CRITERIA

For a sample of completed pencil and paper tests, each question was first scored independently by two judges. A meeting was then held, differences discussed and a final set of criteria agreed. Scripts were then re-scored according to these criteria.

Example of scoring for particular criteria

For example, the tasks in Figs 2 and 3 (see Chapter 1) were designed to assess knowledge and understanding of the ideas expressed in the following objectives devised by Teacher Joan:

- *Teacher 'Joan' - objective 2*

  children should understand that an electric current consists of electrons moving in one direction

- *Teacher 'Joan' - objective 3*

  children should understand that the electrons are moved by a push which is provided by the battery

- *Teacher 'Joan' - objective 4*

  children should understand that the size of this push is indicated by voltage.

The criteria for awarding a 0, 1 or 2 for the child's understanding of the idea in objective 2 are shown in Table 10. Hence, the child's pre-teaching response in Fig 2 was given a score of 1 and the post-teaching response a score of 2.

Table 10 Criteria for test scores (the meaning of 'electric current')	
criteria	**score awarded**
If the child shows no understanding of the meaning of 'electric current'	0
If there is mention of electrons/particles *or* of a flow around a pathway	1
If there is mention of electrons/particles *and* of movement in one (same) direction along a complete pathway	2

Similarly, the criteria for scoring the child's understanding of the ideas in objectives 3 and 4 are shown in Table 11. The pre- and post-teaching responses shown in Fig 3 led to the award of scores of 0 and 2 respectively for this particular child.

Table 11 Criteria for test scores (battery's push is shown by the voltage)	
criteria	**score awarded**
If the child shows no understanding of 'V' or of the role of the battery	0
If the child knows that 'V' stands for voltage	1
If the child recognises 'V' as a measure of the battery's push and knows that 6 V is more push than 1.5 V.	2

When making a judgment about a child's understanding, the researchers relied mainly, but not solely, on the child's response to a particular situation - account was also often taken of responses to other test questions.

Interviews were scored using the same criteria, but with more in-depth evidence and hence greater confidence. The procedures used for analysing the interviews are described in Chapter 6 and in Appendix III.

APPENDIX III

SAMPLE FROM PUPIL INTERVIEW TRANSCRIPTS AND EXAMPLE OF A SUMMARY SHEET

Teacher: Joan; Child Lyn's pre-teaching responses to the 'Julie' situation

dialogue
(I = interviewer; C = child)

analysis

_____ = *preconception*

⬯ = *already known*

▭ = *missing*

I: Next is Julie with her X-ray specs. You said you thought you'd see electricity running past and it would look all sparkly. Can you tell me a bit more about that?

C: Well I don't know, like when it's sparkly - when it's fireworks. I thought of fireworks looking sparkly and wavy and things.

electricity is sparkly / wavy in the wires

I: In the wire? And it would be running past? (C: Yes.) Quickly - or what? (C: Quickly, yes) Sort of pretty quick? (C: Yes.) How quick? (C: Pretty fast, yes.) OK and then the bulb you said you think you'd see two metal bits with a small metal thing inside and electricity rushing everywhere around the bulb. So again sparks?

electricity travels fast

electricity rushes round inside the bulb's metal bit and that brings light

C: Yes - trying to get out of the bulb - that's what I thought.

I: How did the sparks get into the bulb from the wire?

C: Through the metal bit at the end - that bit at the bottom of the bulb (I: Which way?) Um I'm not actually that sure - I think it just goes through the metal bit of the wire inside and it touches the other bit of metal and that sends sparks through that and then it goes ...

'metal bit' inside bulb (= filament?)

I: So the sparks go up to the metal bit of the bulb and then what?

C: And then it sparks in these metal bits - and that brings light.

no particle model for how bulb lights

I: Are the sparks going towards the bulb in both wires or just going in one of the wires or what? You know, from the battery to the bulb?

C: Um, from both wires.

clashing currents idea

I: You think it goes through both of the wires and into the bulb? (C: Yes.) That's interesting. Now what about what's happening inside the battery? (*reads*) You think 'the electricity is trying to get out'. How do you see this electricity? Is it your old sparkler friends again?

C: Yes it's trapped and it can't get out. It's trying to find a way out.

battery is a source of electricity (it's 'trapped inside')

I: What do you mean? Is it a sort of push or burst out or ...? (C: Yes.) Really? Why is it doing that?

C: I don't know. It's been trapped in there and it just wants to get out.

I: So the only way it can get out is - how? (C: By the wires.) If the wires are not there, it stays trapped does it? (C: Yes.) OK.

134

Teacher: Joan; Child Lyn's post-teaching responses to the 'Julie' situation

Key to analysis:

- Ideas are acquired successfully (*S*), partially (*P*), incorrectly (*I*), not at all (*N*), ideas remain unchanged (*U*) or there is a chance for their development (*CFD*).
- Child's reasons for learning an idea are written in BLOCK CAPITALS

I: This is Julie looking inside things with the X-ray specs. You said (*pre-teaching*) she'd see (*reads from test*) 'electrons everywhere going in different directions like dots'. Would you like to add to that?	*P* particle model for conductor (electron motion)
C: Not really because I think dots are going everywhere and then going - they are going in one direction but they are trying to get out like.	*P* particle model for current
I: Why do they go in one direction?	
C: They don't really but, when it (*points to cell*) gives it the push.	
I: When the battery gives it a push they go in one direction? (C: Yes.) How did you learn that, again?	*S* battery pushes electrons
C: When Mrs Bloggs drew the picture on the flip-chart.	TEACHER'S DRAWING
I: The one with all the dots in ? (C: Yes.) And then it showed the arrow with all the dots moving? (C: Yes.) Anything about that you are a bit stuck on? (C: No.) Before the lessons you said she'd see electricity running past and it would look all sparkly. So in what way do you think your ideas have changed?	(VISUAL AID)
C: Well I think still about the sparkly dots and sometimes see things that are sparkly dots ...	*P* particle model for wire
I: But before they were just sparkly but now you think that are dots which are sparkly? (C: Yes.) And you didn't talk about directions, although you did say 'running past' didn't you?	
C: Yes, I thought it just ran straight through it. I didn't think it went slowly or anything - I thought it went fast all the way through it.	*S* electron speed varies
I: You think now it goes slowly do you? (C: Yes.) That's interesting. What happened to make you think that? How did you learn that?	
C: I don't think it goes really slowly but I don't think it goes that fast.	
I: It's an interesting change but you can't remember what it was that the teacher said or did? Did she tell you that?	
C: I can't remember. No, I don't think so.	CAN'T REMEMBER
I: You just think that's what happens - they move more slowly? (C: Yes.) Anything you are unsure about with that? (C: No.) OK inside the bulb you said (*reads*) 'electrons burning up to make the light.' Can you tell me more? What do you mean by that?	

C: There is a little bit of metal inside the bulb and I just think when it goes   *U metal bit inside bulb*
   light it has nowhere else to go and it just burns up and it makes light.   *I electrons burn up to*
                                                                                   make light
I: OK, how did you learn that? Anything the teacher did or said?
C: I don't think so. I think I just thought of that for myself.   CHILD'S DEDUCTION
I: Nothing that you did in the lessons made you think of that, that you
   can remember? (C: No.) Anything about that you are unsure of or are
   stuck on? (C: No.) Before the lesson you thought (*reads*) 'inside the
   bulb two metal bits with small metal things inside and the electricity
   rushing everywhere around the bulb.' In what way do you think
   your ideas have changed?
C: A lot because I didn't think of that really. There is something in the
   lesson that made me think of that but (I: What - electrons burning up
   to make light?) Yes but I can't remember.   CAN'T REMEMBER
I: Quite a change isn't it? (C: Yes.) Do you think you might have
   thought of that yourself or was it something the teacher told you
   (C: What?) - what you think now, electrons burning up.
C: I think somebody gave me the idea. I think Mrs Bloggs may have   CHILD'S DEDUCTION
   said something that made me think of that but I'm not quite sure.   FROM TEACHER'S
I: Finally what's happening inside the battery - you thought Julie would   WORDS
   see 'the battery just pushing the electrons along'. Can you add to that?
C: Trying to get out I think.   *I battery a source of*
I: Out of the battery?   *electrons*
C: Yes, the electrons pushing, trying to get out and find a way out and ...   *N electrons already*
I: OK. How did you learn that do you think?   *in the wire*
C: About the bicycle chain. When it goes round it's exactly the same like   BICYCLE CHAIN
   um ... when they come out they all being pushed along together.   ANALOGY
I: Rather than one pushing the next one and the next one pushing the
   next one?
C: Yes, they are all going round at the same time.   *S all electrons move*
I: OK. The bicycle obviously made an impression on you didn't it?   *instantaneously*
   (C: yes.) It was helpful? (C: Yes.) Anything about that you are unsure
   about? (C: No.) OK before teaching you thought this (reads): 'electricity
   inside the battery trying to get out, so in what way do you think your
   ideas have changed?
C: Well I still think it's trying to get out - the electrons are trying to get   *I electrons try to get*
   out there but the electricity won't.   *out of battery*
I: But you have added this idea of electrons haven't you, and the idea   *+*
   of the battery pushing. (C: Yes.) Can you think what it was that   *S battery pushes*
   changed your idea about the battery?   *electrons*
C: I think it's something I did but I can't remember what.

EXAMPLE OF A CHILD'S SUMMARY SHEET

(i) Pre-teaching and post-teaching ideas

Pre-teaching   PUPIL: Lyn   TEACHER: Joan

Ideas acquired

(S=successfully; P=partially; I=incorrectly; N=not acquired; U=unchanged idea; CFD=chance for development)

Pre-teaching

Preconceptions
- battery is a source of electricity
- electricity is trapped inside the battery trying to get out
- wires wrap around the bulb and battery holders (procedural knowledge)

- electricity flows through the wires in a certain direction

- consumption model (evident post-teaching)
- clashing currents model; (electricity goes from the battery to the bulb)
- light is caused by sparks rushing around the bulb's metal bit inside
- light generated when electricity touches metal at bottom of bulb
- current is 'sparkly wavy lines' going fast from one place to another in wire
- voltage measures how much power (electricity) the battery has
- bulb brightness is affected by the power of the battery
- 2 bulbs in series are dimmer than 1 alone because they share the electricity
- electricity goes through metal but not other things

- in parallel means electricity's spread out, passes through everything

Missing
- no particle model of why bulb lights up
- no particle model for conductors and insulators
- no particle model for electricity

- parallel circuits are better because bulbs are brighter than when in series

- parallel circuits are better because if 1 bulb is removed the other still works
- knowledge of symbol for a bulb (guessed)
- correct orientation of a cell symbol
- knowledge of a LED

- how to connect (procedural knowledge), represent a parallel circuit
- current in a series circuit
- knowledge of an ammeter (inferred)

Knows
- complete pathway idea
- how to connect up a MES bulb (unsure - admitted post-teaching)
- bulb still lights up if battery leads are reversed
- real-life circuits are shown by circuit diagrams
- little bit of metal inside bulb 'goes light'
- factual knowledge of conducting ('things like metal') and insulating substances

Ideas acquired

- S   *battery pushes electrons*
- I   battery is a source of electrons - 'inside battery trying to get out'
- S   *leads plug in to the battery and bulb holders*
- I   wires are essential for to make a circuit (direct connections not OK)
- S   *electrons travel in the wires, with varying speed*
- S   *movement of electrons (electricity) are the same 'all the way around the full circuit'*
- I   electrons burn up in bulb to make light

- P   *current is electrons ('sparkly dots') moving through the wires*
- S   *voltage indicates the push of the battery*
- S   *bulb brightness depends on the push from the battery*
- I   electrons are shared between two bulbs in a series circuit
- P   *language - knows 'conductor' and 'insulator' but can't recall which is which*
- S   *salt water is a conductor*
- P   meaning of in parallel (i.e. really 2 independent circuits) - just procedural K

- P   particle model for bulb ("metal in bulb lights when she gets electrons")
- P   metals let electrons (electricity) pass through, other substances don't
- S   *electrons don't always go in 1 direction - go 'everywhere' until given a push*
- S   *electrons are already in the wires (inferred from above)*
- S   *in parallel is better because bulbs are brighter than when in series*
- N   bulbs in parallel circuits are equally bright
- S   *in parallel is better because 1 bulb works if other is removed*
- N   knowledge of symbols for cell and bulb
- S   *correct orientation of a cell symbol*
- S   *language - = LED means 'light emitting diode'*
- P   *LED is a one way system (procedural K rather than 'one-way conductor')*
- S   *how to connect up, represent a parallel circuit (procedural K)*
- N, CFD   less current for 2 bulbs in a series circuit than for 1 bulb alone
- P   ammeter measures push of battery and power
- N   language - name of ammeter

- U   complete pathway idea
- I   how to connect MES bulb (both wires to base of bulb)
-   (no information about this, post-teaching)
- U   real-life circuits are shown by circuit diagrams
- U   little bit of metal inside bulb 'goes light'
- I   water is not a conductor, string is a conductor

Note:) brackets indicate linked pre-teaching ideas; (brackets show linked post-teaching ideas.
Ideas successfully acquired post-teaching are shown in italics

APPENDIX III (contd)

EXAMPLE OF A CHILD'S SUMMARY SHEET

(ii) Child's reasons for his/her learning (Child: Lyn; Teacher: Joan)

Action	Learning
• child tried something else because of previous doubts (no teacher influence)	*Incorrect method of connecting MES bulb (both wires to bottom of bulb) - did it correctly pre-teaching but was unsure!*
• teacher talking	*Wire takes electrons to the bulb*
• can't remember	*Electrons are like little dots* *Electrons go slowly*
• inference from other knowledge (motion of electrons when no current)	*Electric current is electrons moving through wire*
• child's deduction from teacher's words	*Electrons burn up to make light inside a little bit of metal within the bulb*
• bicycle chain analogy (partially understood)	*Battery pushes electrons (like pedals),* *Electrons push, trying to get out of the battery,* *All the electrons are pushed at the same time,* *The same thing is happening in all the wires of the circuit (because the chain stays the same),*
• teacher showing diagram	*Electrons 'go everywhere' in the wire and go in one direction when pushed by battery*
• child 'doing something'	*The battery pushes*
• experimenting	*Metal lets electrons through* *String, salt water make the bulb light (conduct) water won't make the bulb light (i.e insulates)* *LED is a one-way system with electricity*
• building circuits	*Parallel circuits better because bulbs are brighter* *'Parallel' refers to the way you connect the wires (i.e. procedural knowledge - not conceptual)*
• using an ammeter	*The electrons are the same all round the circuit,* *An ammeter measures battery push and power*

(this child not asked how she learned her knowledge of circuit diagrams)

(iii) Child's test scores (Child: Lyn; Teacher: Joan)

Teacher's objectives:	Child's score	
	Pre-teaching	Post teaching
1. an electric circuit is a pathway which must be complete for a current to be present,	2	2
2. an electric current consists of electrons moving in one direction,	0	2
3. the push to move the electrons is provided by the battery,	0	2
4. the size of the push is indicated by voltage.	0	2
5. some substances (conductors) allow an electric current to be present and others (insulators) do not,	1	2
6. a diode is a one-way conductor of electricity.	0	1
7. there are two ways of connecting components: in series and in parallel,	0	2
8. in parallel is better because bulbs are brighter than when in series (when connected to the same battery).	0	2
9. real-life circuits can be represented by circuit diagrams with symbols acting for components,	2	2

138

APPENDIX IV

COMPARISON OF SCORES ON PENCIL AND PAPER TESTS WITH INTERVIEW SCORES

Mean scores for each sub-group of six children

(i)   Teacher Joan (six Year 7 children)

Teacher's objectives (see Chapter 3 for details)	Pre-teaching		Post-teaching	
	Test	Interview	Test	Interview
1.	2	2	2	2
2.	0	0.17	1.5	1.33
3.	0	0	2	2
4.	0.33	0	2	2
5.	1	1.17	1.33	1.67
6.	0.17	0.17	1.83	1.67
7.	0.67	0.67	2	2
8.	0.17	0.17	1.67	1.83
9.	0.83	1.67	1.83	2.

(ii)   Teacher Lucy (six Year 6 children)

Teacher's objectives (see Chapter 4 for details)	Pre-teaching		Post-teaching	
	Test	Interview	Test	Interview
1.	1	1	1.5	1.67
2.	1	0.5	1.33	1.33
3.	0	0	0.33	0.33
4.	0.83	0.83	1.17	1.5
5.	0.17	0.17	0.83	0.83
6.	1.33	1.33	1.67	1.67

(iii)   Teacher Sarah (six Year 6 children)

Teacher's objectives (see Chapter 5 for details)	Pre-teaching		Post-teaching	
	Test	Interview	Test	Interview
1.	1.17	2	1.5	2
2.	0.5	1.33	1.5	2
3.	0	0	0.67	1.5
4.	0	0	1	2
5.	0	0	1.33	2
6.	0	0	1.33	1.33
7.	0	0	0.33	0
8.	0.5	0	1.17	0.67
9.	0	0	1.3	1.5
10.	1	1.17	1.17	2
11.	0.83	2	1.83	2
12.	0	0	0.5	1
13.	0	0	0.5	0.5
14.	2	2	2	2

APPENDIX V

FURTHER TEACHING KNOWLEDGE USED BY SARAH

This teaching knowledge was used by Sarah at the beginning of Session 4 to convey ideas which she had not originally planned to teach, so its effectiveness was not tested directly during the research. It is a sound approach but the children's low scores for a simpler related idea suggest that it was ineffective. This is discussed in the Commentary in Chapter 5.

Sarah first pointed out the path of electrons through the bulb on a large diagram (Fig 43) and explained this in terms of water going through a pipe, with a constriction which was likened to the bulb's filament:

Teacher: This picture is meant to be like a pipe - if it goes narrow what happens to how well the water can flow through the pipe? Is it going to be easier or harder to flow through the narrow bit?

Children: Harder.

Teacher: OK. If there is a narrow part, the water is going to find it harder to push its way through - it's going to slow the water down. It's a little bit like that with the light bulb. The electrons move easily in the big thick copper wire but when they start moving through the thin bit - we call it the filament - made of something different, the electrons have trouble moving through.

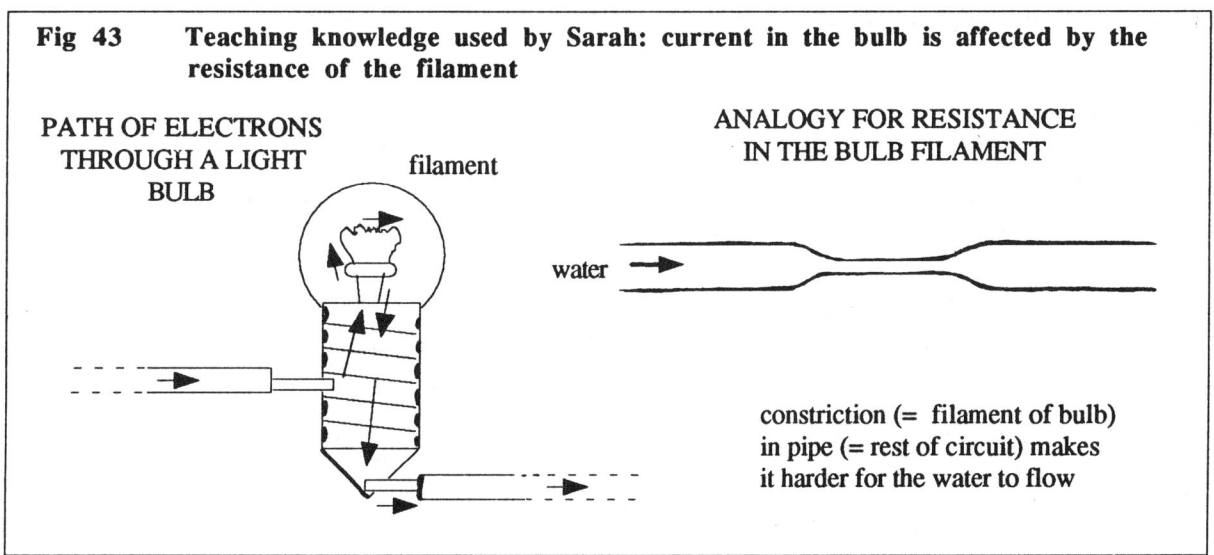

Fig 43   Teaching knowledge used by Sarah: current in the bulb is affected by the resistance of the filament

PATH OF ELECTRONS THROUGH A LIGHT BULB

ANALOGY FOR RESISTANCE IN THE BULB FILAMENT

filament

water

constriction (= filament of bulb) in pipe (= rest of circuit) makes it harder for the water to flow

This suggests that electrons move fast in the wires and slow down due to the resistance of the filament - a misconception. In fact electrons pass through the filament faster then through the wires so that the *rate* of electron flow (i.e. the current) is the same throughout the circuit - see Summers, Kruger and Mant (1995) for a full discussion of this point.

Sarah explained the heating and lighting effect of the bulb in terms of electrons colliding with the atoms of the filament:

Teacher: .. so what scientists think happens is that the electrons are bumping into atoms in that filament and causing them to vibrate and that is what is making the heat and light come off the filament - that's what's making the light glow - the electrons are having a hard time moving through the filament.

She now re-visited the bicycle chain analogy and tried to show the children what happens when the electrons (i.e. the links) encounter a resistance, in the way that the water does in the narrow part of the pipe. This resistance took the form of a piece of folded paper which was pressed against the chain as it moved:

Teacher: If you put the paper against the chain, what will happen?
Dean: It might stop.
Leah: It will slow down.
Teacher: Susan, keep pushing (the pedal by) the same (amount). You're like the battery - you've only got so much push in you (*she places the paper to rub against the chain*). What happened?
Susan: It slowed down.
Teacher: So it restricted the movement of the chain, just like the thin bit of pipe restricted the movement of the water and the thin bit of wire was restricting the movement of the electrons. The whole thing, all the electrons, was moving more slowly.

Note how Sarah rightly emphasised the effect of the resistance on *the whole circuit*. The 'real-life' equivalent of this was shown as a series circuit in which an extra bulb was added (Fig 44).

Fig 44   Teaching knowledge used by Sarah: developing the bicycle chain analogy to illustrate the effect of adding an extra bulb in series

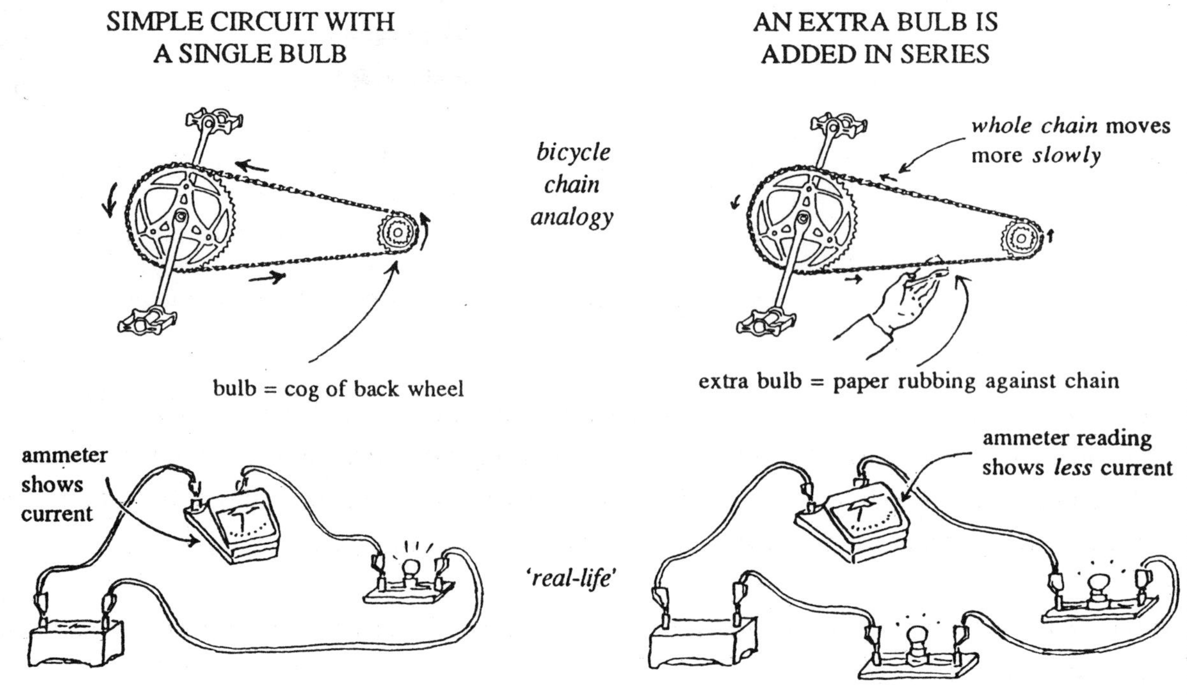

SIMPLE CIRCUIT WITH A SINGLE BULB

AN EXTRA BULB IS ADDED IN SERIES

bicycle chain analogy

whole chain moves more slowly

bulb = cog of back wheel

extra bulb = paper rubbing against chain

ammeter shows current

ammeter reading shows *less* current

'real-life'

Children were asked to predict what would happen to the ammeter reading (i.e. the size of the current in the circuit) when this bulb was added in series. Sarah showed the effect of doing this in terms of her 'water-in-a-pipe' analogy (Fig 45):

Teacher: When we add another light bulb it's like this. Another restriction. What might happen to our ammeter reading which tells you how much current there is?

Sandy: It might go down a bit.

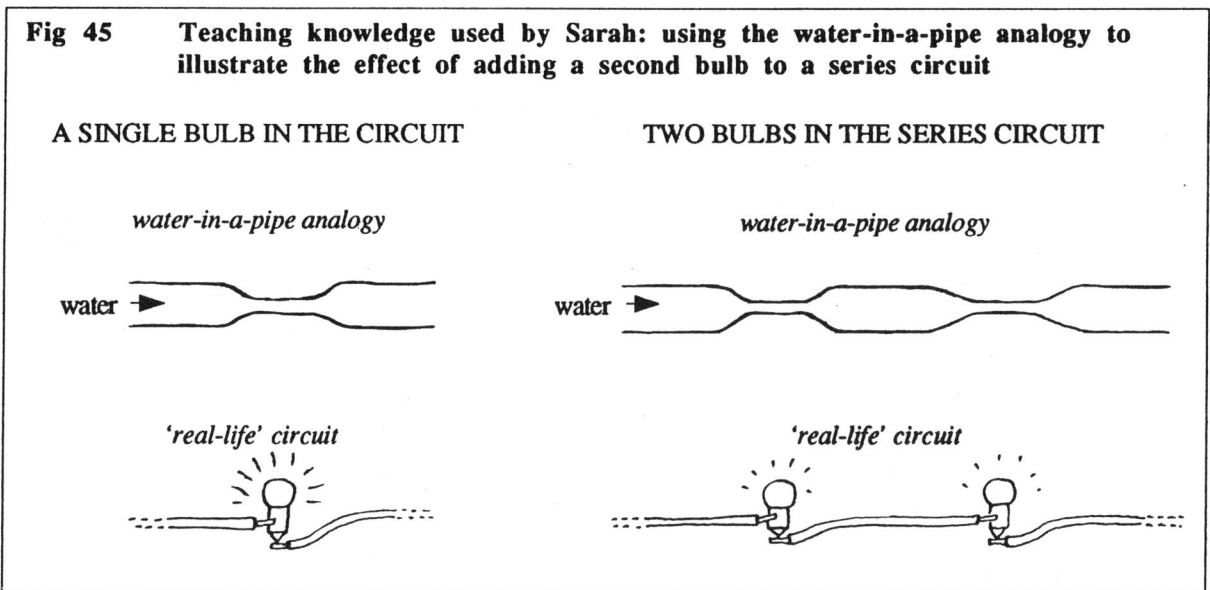

Fig 45   **Teaching knowledge used by Sarah: using the water-in-a-pipe analogy to illustrate the effect of adding a second bulb to a series circuit**

A SINGLE BULB IN THE CIRCUIT

TWO BULBS IN THE SERIES CIRCUIT

water-in-a-pipe analogy

water-in-a-pipe analogy

water ➤

water ➤

'real-life' circuit

'real-life' circuit

An explanation was then given in terms of the bicycle chain analogy:

Teacher: Because if it (i.e. *the ammeter reading*) does (become less), the electrons have got another hard bit to go through - that's two things restricting the movement of the electrons - (like) me putting my piece of paper on the chain and Michael pressing another piece of paper at the other end. That's two things to restrict the movement of the chain.

Sarah made a slight error here: with her and Michael pressing paper on the chain the total number of resistances (bulbs) represented is three, not two, since the wheel's back cog is also a resistance to movement of the chain and so represents a bulb. She explained this 3-bulb circuit in terms of her water-in-a-pipe analogy before moving on to 'another kind of circuit' - parallel circuits.

Parallel circuits were explained in terms of water leaving a tank - a variant of an analogy that Sarah had encountered in her training (Fig 46):

Teacher: Here is a big tank of water. If I put a hole in it (*draws on board*), what's going to happen?

Gary: Water comes out.

Teacher: If I put another hole here, same size, (*draws*) what will happen? The tank will empty - how?

143

Michelle:	Fast.
Teacher:	How many times as fast?
Gary:	Twice as fast.
Teacher:	OK. We've got more places for the water to go. More can come through because it's got more outlets so it will empty quicker. It's like that with the battery as well. The electrons can go this way or this way - they've got 2 chances - so these can be moving round much quicker. So what we find is that the amount of electric current, of electrons moving, is greater when we add an extra bulb in parallel because there are more choices of pathway for the electrons to move along.

Fig 46   **An analogy for electric current in a parallel circuit (taught to Sarah during her training) - 'Emptying a tank'**

Analogy

The water tank will empty more quickly when two drainage pipes in parallel are used rather than just one pipe on its own.

Current in P will increase as more drainage tubes are added in parallel

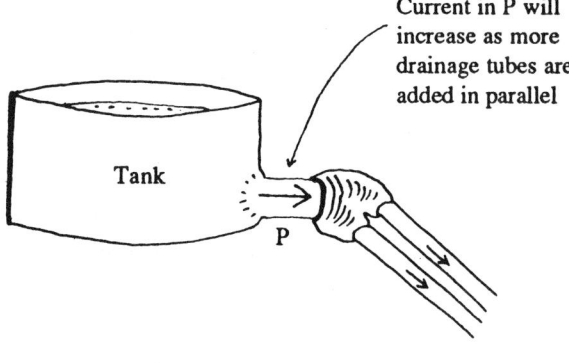

Tank

P

'Real-life' circuit

Current here increases as bulbs are added in parallel

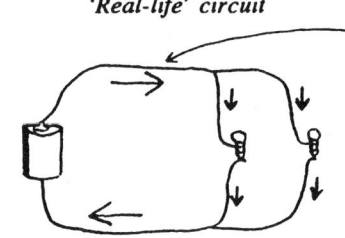

Circuit diagram

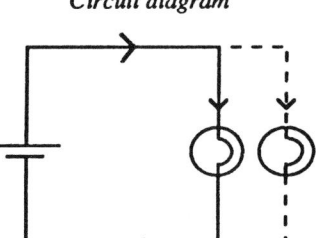

Note: Like all analogies, this has its limitations. It clearly shows how each tube added (= branch of a parallel circuit) 'draws' extra water through pipe P (= current in the battery leads). However, it can also convey the scientifically incorrect idea that electricity (= water) is stored in the battery (= the tank), rather than being already present (as electrons) in the wires.

An improved version of this analogy, incorporating a pump which takes into account the battery's role as a 'pusher' of the electrons, can be seen in Fig 26, Chapter 4.

APPENDIX VI

ANALOGIES FOR ELECTRIC CIRCUITS

Appropriate analogies are a very important part of subject specific teaching knowledge. On page 36, when commenting on Joan's teaching, we discussed the bicycle chain analogy in some detail. In this appendix analogies are discussed further, and a different analogy which teachers can use in primary school classrooms is described.

Key features

A good analogy for primary school science will capture as many as possible of the following features of a simple electric circuit:

- electricity is made up of electrons (the analogy should help with the notion of electricity as particles).
- the electrons (the electricity) are already in the wires and components - the electricity (electrons) does not come from the battery.
- the battery provides the 'push' to make the electrons move.
- the electrons round the circuit all start moving at the same time.
- the electrons all move in one direction to form a current.
- electricity (electrons) are not used up as they pass through the bulb i.e. there is the same current both sides of the bulb.
- the moving electrons (the current) are the means by which energy is transferred to the bulb from the battery.
- hence it is energy which is 'used up' (transferred to the bulb), not electrons or current.
- the energy is transferred to the bulb though collisions between the moving electrons and the fixed atoms inside the bulb filament.
- a battery becomes 'flat' when it can no longer push the electrons i.e. the push drops.

The bicycle chain analogy (Fig 47) captures most of these features successfully, except perhaps for the idea of 'something' (energy) being transferred to the bulb. An alternative, which includes this feature in a more obvious way, is described below.

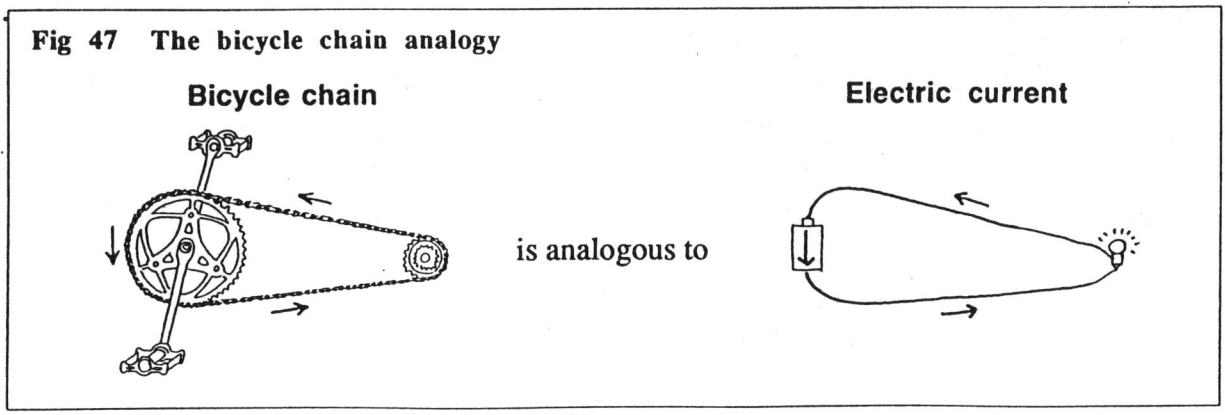

Fig 47   The bicycle chain analogy

Bicycle chain   Electric current

is analogous to

The 'pupils and sweets' chain

This analogy, which is acted out easily in the classroom, is shown in Fig 48.

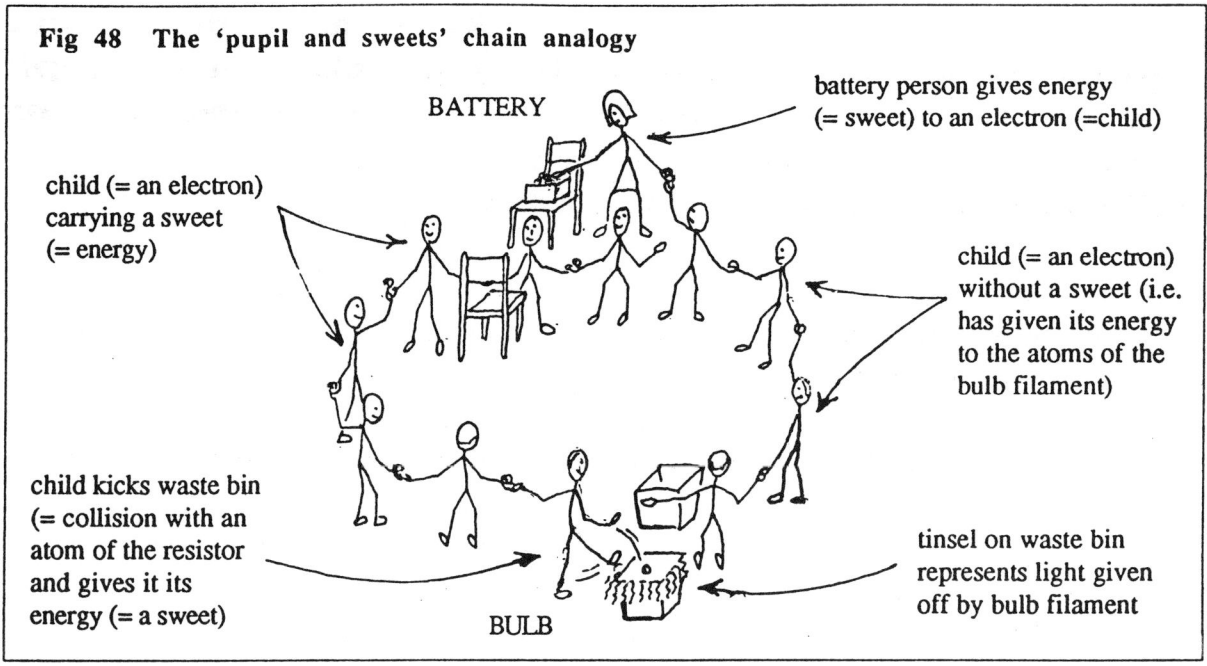

Fig 48   The 'pupil and sweets' chain analogy

BATTERY

battery person gives energy (= sweet) to an electron (=child)

child (= an electron) carrying a sweet (= energy)

child (= an electron) without a sweet (i.e. has given its energy to the atoms of the bulb filament)

child kicks waste bin (= collision with an atom of the resistor and gives it its energy (= a sweet)

tinsel on waste bin represents light given off by bulb filament

BULB

The roles and actions are as follows:

- the pupils (the electrons or electricity) form a large circle and link hands.
- the pair of chairs between which the pupils will move is the battery.
- a box of sweets on one of the chairs is the stored energy of the battery.
- the pair of waste bins, through which the pupils will move, is the bulb.
- the 'battery person' shouts go and all pupils start moving *at the same time.*
- every time a pupil passes between the chairs the 'battery person' gives the pupil a sweet.
- when pupils pass though the waste bins they kick one (i.e. collide with atoms of the bulb filament) and drop their sweet into one of the bins (i.e. give the atom energy).
- the emission of light can be shown by means of tinsel draped on the bin.

The strength of this analogy is that the energy transfer mechanism is very evident - the battery runs down because the sweets run out and energy is transferred to the bins ('used up' or 'consumed'). At the same time, the 'pupil current' (the moving electricity) is clearly not used up but is the means of energy transfer. Also the collision mechanism is represented.

Possible weaknesses of the analogy are:

- there is no obvious push from the battery

- the fact that pupils all have to move at the same time is a bit artificial i.e. it is not something that *has* to happen (whereas this is the case for the bicycle chain).

Which of these analogies is best?

The answer to this is that, like all analogies, both have strengths and weaknesses. However, we believe that either the bicycle chain or the pupil sweet chain are helpful ways of helping children make sense of simple circuits and are a useful platform for further work at secondary school.

Is there a better analogy?

The answer is yes: it is known as the *gravitational analogy* and it is shown in outline in Fig 49.

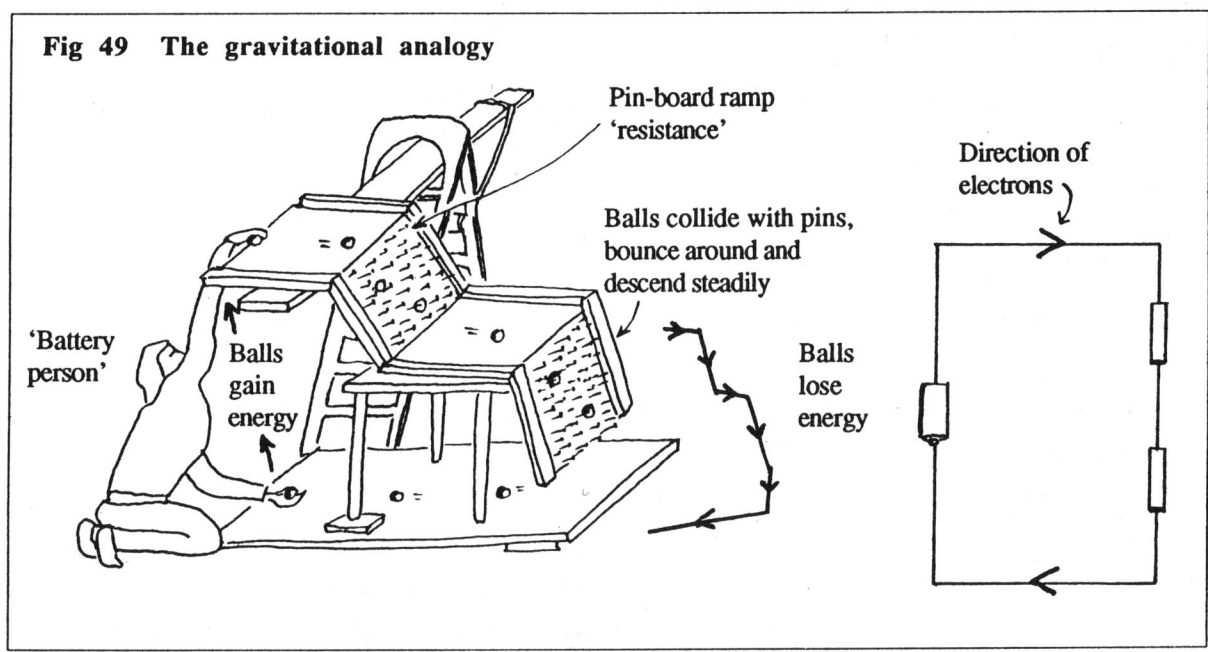

Fig 49   The gravitational analogy

Pin-board ramp 'resistance'

Balls collide with pins, bounce around and descend steadily

Direction of electrons

'Battery person'

Balls gain energy

Balls lose energy

The full scientific view of a simple circuit needs the concept of an electric field, and this can be understood through thinking about the role of the Earth's gravitational field in the model on the left hand side of Fig 49. However, an obvious difficulty is that the analogy relies on a prior understanding of the Earth's gravitational field and, in fact, of the concept of gravitational potential energy.

A detailed description of this gravitational analogy is beyond the scope of this book. However, if you would like to know more about it, an account written especially for primary school teachers can be found in *Current Understanding: electricity concepts and practice for priamry and non-specialist secondary teacher education* (Summers, Kruger and Mant, 1995).

A 'marble run' gravitational analogy

Marble runs are a popular and readily available toy (e.g. from Galt Toys, The Early Learning

Centre) which can perhaps already be found in many primary schools. A simple gravitational model of an electric circuit can be built with a marble run as shown in Fig 50.

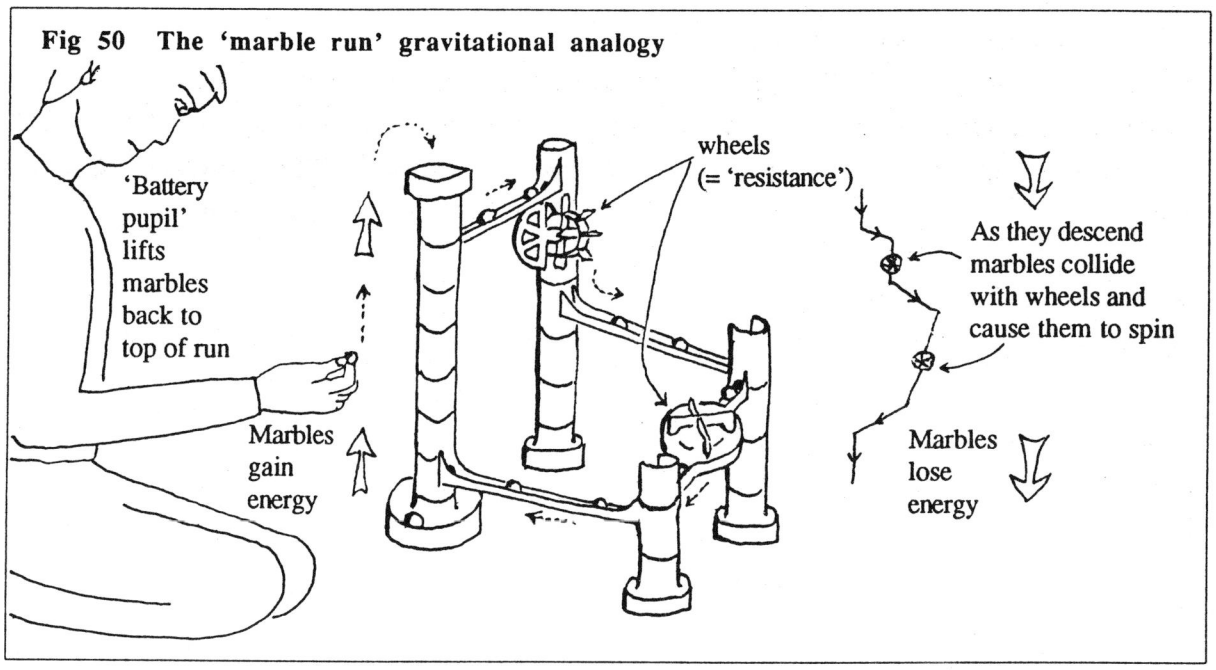

Fig 50   The 'marble run' gravitational analogy

What happens in the model?

- Initially marbles are placed all along the run and held in place by pupils.
- When the teacher says 'go' the pupils release the marbles.
- All the marbles start to move simultaneously.
- The marbles travel from top to bottom of the run pulled by gravity.
- On the way they collide with two wheels and cause the wheels to spin.
- When the marbles reach the bottom they are lifted back to the top of the run by a pupil.

What does it represent?

- The marbles represent electrons in the wires already.
- Starting the marbles moving represents connecting up the circuit.
- The moving marbles pulled by gravity represent the electric current made up of electrons pushed by the battery.
- When the marbles hit a wheel and make it move, this represents the elctrons passing through a bulb and colliding with the fixed atoms in the filament, causing them to vibrate and hence produce light and heating.
- The child lifting the marbles back to the top of the run represents the battery.

APPENDIX VII

CURRENT DIRECTION - CONVENTIONAL
OR ELECTRON CURRENT?

Experience of INSET courses suggests that participants are often confused about current direction. This is because

(i)   they are told that the direction of the *conventional current* in a circuit is from the positive pole of the battery to the negative pole, and

(ii)   that the current really consists of electrons moving in the opposite direction i.e. from the negative to the positive pole of the battery. This is the *electron current.*

The situation is summarised in Fig 51.

These two terms - conventional current and electron current - can give rise to the misconception that there are two currents. This is, of course, not the case. There is only one current and it consists of electrons moving from the negative to the positive pole of the battery.

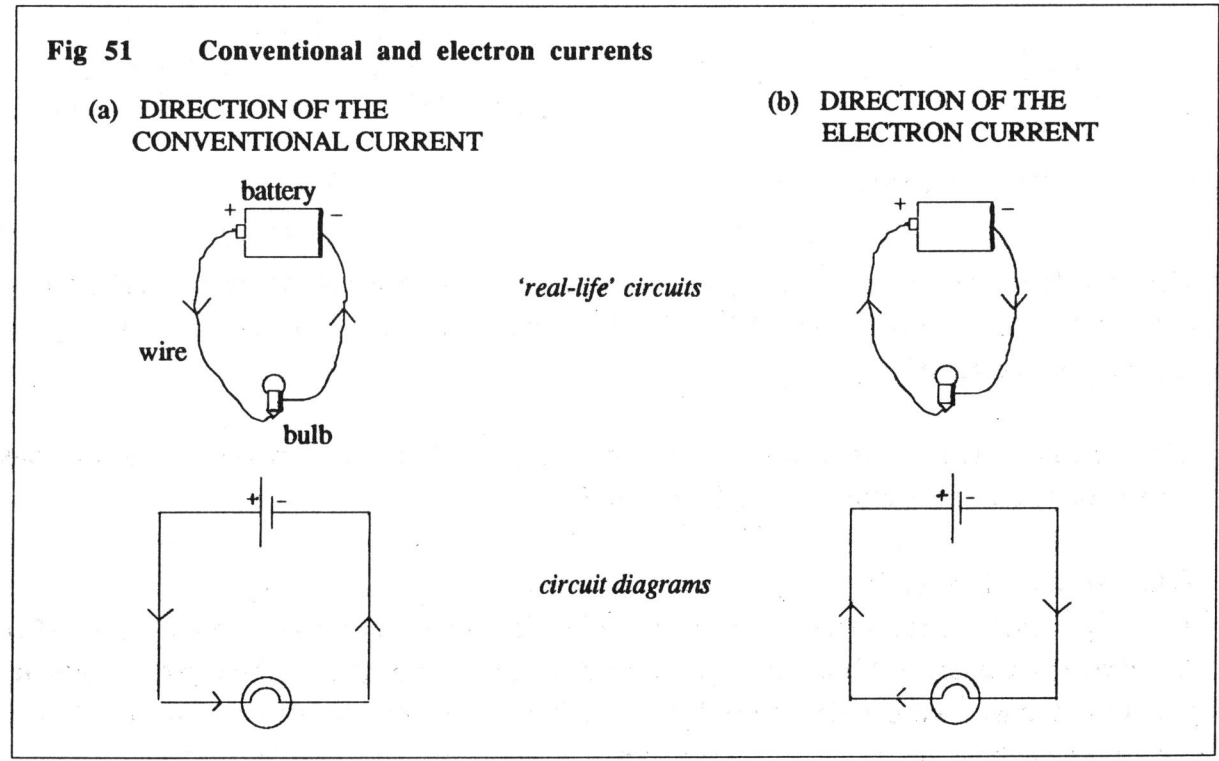

Fig 51   Conventional and electron currents

(a) DIRECTION OF THE CONVENTIONAL CURRENT

(b) DIRECTION OF THE ELECTRON CURRENT

'real-life' circuits

circuit diagrams

Why, then, is the term conventional current ever used?

The answer is a historical one. Scientists had developed the idea of something flowing in a circuit (the current) long before the electron was discovered. Not knowing exactly what was flowing, they assumed a direction of flow from the positive to the negative battery pole. Even today, nearly all books, scientists, engineers and electricians use this conventional current direction (Fig 51a).

An analogy

Suppose you have a central heating radiator. Your knowledge of central heating systems is very limited and all you know is that hot water passes through the radiator, but you don't know the direction.

You might assume for years that it flows from A to B (Fig 52a): this is your conventional current.

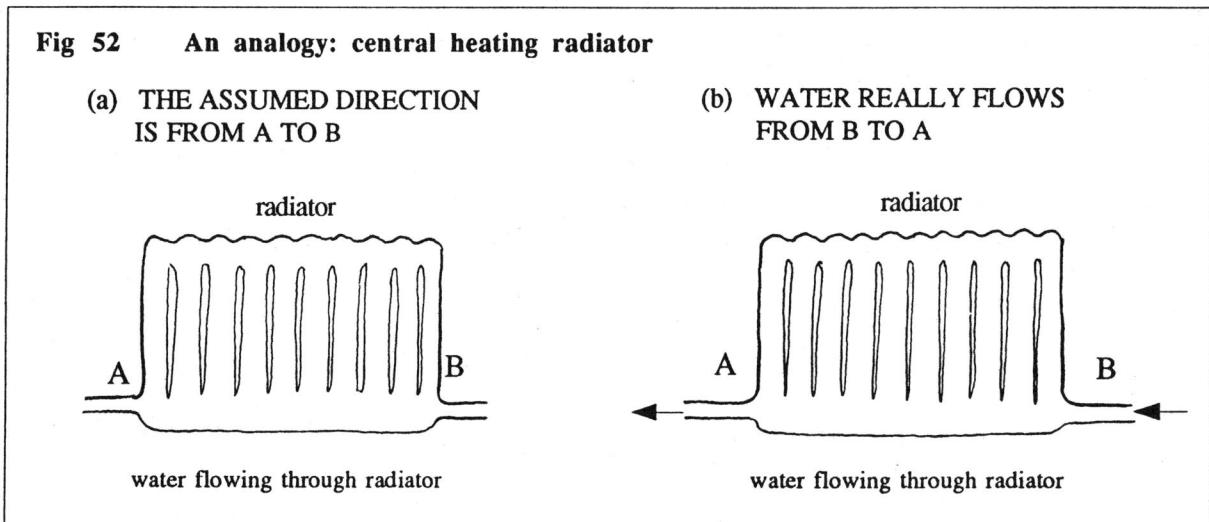

Fig 52   An analogy: central heating radiator

(a) THE ASSUMED DIRECTION IS FROM A TO B

(b) WATER REALLY FLOWS FROM B TO A

Then one day you learn more about your central heating system and discover that really the water is flowing from B to A (Fig 52b)! This is the water current - the real current (analogous to the electron current).

However, as far as the heating effect is concerned, the direction is not important and you could quite happily go on assuming a flow from A to B.

What should I teach?

At primary level, the fact that the current has a direction is probably more important than what that direction actually is. However, if you are teaching about electrons and a current as moving electrons, it makes sense to define the direction of the current as that of the moving electrons. This is the electron current i.e. from the negative to the positive pole of the battery.

At secondary school children will learn about conventional current. Careful teaching will then be necessary to avoid the misconception that there are two currents.